Seven Lives on Salt River

'I have never been in a small town that had not a few distinctive spirits.'

— Jane Mander, *Sun* newspaper, 1922.

'And when he saw Pahi he said to the captain, "I like the look of this place. I'll land here."'

— Jane Mander, *Allen Adair*

'We found on inquiry that little or nothing was known in Auckland of Te Pahi . . . a newspaper wrote of the Kaipara under the title of Terra Incognita.'

— W.D. Hay, *Brighter Britain*, 1882.

Pampered environment. A Pahi river idyll, Stevens landing, The Pines.

Seven Lives
on Salt River

Dick Scott

REED ◆ SOUTHERN CROSS

AUCKLAND

For Rosie and Mark
labourers in the field

The author gratefully acknowledges assistance
received from the New Zealand Literary Fund.

Air New Zealand is thanked for providing travel for research.

Published by Reed Books in conjunction with Southern Cross Books, Auckland. Reed Books is
a division of Reed Publishing (NZ) Ltd, 39 Rawene Rd, Birkenhead, Auckland (www.reed.co.nz).
Associated companies, branches and representatives throughout the world.

ISBN 0 7900 0708 8

© 1987 Dick Scott

The author asserts his moral rights in the work.

First published by Hodder & Stoughton 1987
Reprinted 1988
Reprinted by Reed Books 1999

Printed in Hong Kong

Contents

FOREWORD   7

1. THE FATAL COMPACT   11

2. SCHEMES AND DREAMS   29

3. THE GREAT PAHI REGATTA & OTHER DIVERSIONS   43

4. HE MADE THE VINE FLOURISH   57

5. THE COUNT WHO ATE WITH THE CREW   75

6. NO PICNIC AT PURIRI POINT   87

7. ALWAYS A PICNIC AT THE PINES   97

8. THE SILENCING OF FRANK BLACKWELL'S SISTER   109

9. A PARTY OF ONE   125

10. THE COATES FAMILY & THEIR WAYWARD SON   137

A NOTE ON SOURCES   154

ILLUSTRATION CREDITS   158

INDEX   158

1. COATES
2. POOK
3. JACKMAN
4. DE LABROSSE
5. STEVENS
6. BLACKWELL
7. SCOTLAND

Paparoa

Matakohe

Matakohe River

Paparoa Ck

Pahi River

Auté Bay

Metcalfe

Rathbone

Pukehuia

Marahemu

Weber

Adams

Pahi

Whakapirau

Karakanui

Kirikiri Inlet

Arapaoa

Arapaoa River

Page Pt

Whakapirau Ck

Puriri Pt

To Manders

River

Tanoa

Otamatea River

Gittos Mission

Batley

Te Kopua Pt

KAIPARA

HARBOUR

The Funnel

Tinopai

Hargreaves Run

Foreword

This book began as a history of the Pahi region, that isolated network of waterways in the north-east Kaipara that is Jane Mander territory. But her images of mysterious houses in the pines kept recurring, comfortable retreats hidden from the water in Victorian gardens, a boat moored by the jetty. The urge to penetrate such aloof places took over and instead of addressing general themes the book resolved itself round the intimate lives of seven families. That they proved to be extraordinarily diverse in their interests — and behaviour — many exerting an influence on national affairs, was a discovery as unexpected as it was welcome.

A context for those lives is given in three introductory chapters. One looks at the missionary era that delivered undisturbed occupation of the land to white settlers, a second looks at the thwarted hopes of those who planned grand entreprenurial schemes, and the third glances at the social life of the community.

The original suggestion for a history came from the Otamatea Regatta Club who in 1987 celebrate their centenary. I am indebted to the club president, Kerry Bonham, for his readiness to give me freedom of action and for his encouragement and provision of water transport. The club secretary, Owen Stevens and his wife Mary, have given generous hospitality over an extended period and their knowledge and enthusiasm (and far-flung network of contacts) has sustained to a high degree the research, writing and production of the book.

Practical support from the club included arranging grants-in-aid towards the collection of early photographs. The Pahi Reserve Board, guardians of the celebrated Moreton Bay fig, regarded as one of the ten finest exotic trees in New Zealand, was particularly generous in this regard. Helpful contributions were also made by the National Bank of New Zealand and Maungaturoto Rotary Club.

Few written records have survived the wash-house copper fire or, in one case of wholesale destruction, the tide. A knot of Norfolk pines on a headland or a magnolia blooming in a bay is very often the only physical trace left by a community that deserted the harbour when the roads came. It has been necessary to travel thousands of kilometres along those roads in search of oral history and it was only the co-operation of old Kaipara hands that made it possible to flesh-out the story. Many of their names appear in the text, more in reference notes, but since over a hundred people were interviewed it has been impossible to include all who helped. To those who gave time and knowledge — often more than once — I give sincere thanks, with particular gratitude to those who unlocked family histories, family photographs — and family skeletons.

One special act of generosity that must be acknowledged at this point was the gift by Billie Guinness of her father Frank Blackwell's collection of glass negatives. Some three hundred studies of the greatest botanical and historical interest, including original plates from Laing and Blackwell's classic *Plants of New Zealand,* have been deposited with the Auckland Museum.

The farmers who cheerfully let me keep tramping over their land must be thanked. The main sites investigated and their present owners were Jackman's Heathcote (Warren Butterworth); Scotland's Riverside (Ruth and Bill Smellie); Coates's Ruatuna (Miss Joy Aickin) and Te Kawau (Ken and June Weber); Blackwell's Karepo (Neil and Clare McInnes); W.H. Stevens's The Pines (Ted Trembath); the Gittos mission (Trevor and Chrissie Linnell); and the de Labrosse sites, at the head of Pahi River (Shirley and Ted Mooney) and Cloon Even down-river (Owen and Mary Stevens). The Pook site at Puriri Point, as lonely as it ever was, has been unoccupied for 33 years and I trust its many absentee Maori owners will forgive me for often crunching up their shell beach and sitting under the trees.

Warm thanks are due to botanist Dr Robert Cooper who visited abandoned gardens on the Pahi River to identify trees and shrubs. His assistance in unravelling the "mystery" of Ellen Blackwell was also invaluable and permitting me to use a Cockayne anecdote from his own work in progress was typically generous. John Stacpoole, Historic Places Trust architect, made a special journey to inspect The Pines, the only house on the river remaining in original condition apart from well-known Ruatuna. His apparently inexhaustible knowledge of early families was freely shared and among other fertile leads he pointed me in the direction of the long-buried Gittos-Fairburn case. David Simmons, in addition to supplying key information on Ngati Whatua carvings, kindly allowed me to use a photograph from his forthcoming catalogue of Maori material held by the British Museum. Maori elders consulted included Ned Wiapo, Whangarei, Mohi Manukau, Helensville, Blossom Connolly, (nee Manukau), Kaiwaka, and Tokomauri Walker (Waaka), Batley. Their help was invaluable but like all those interviewed, they do not necessarily agree, of course, with what has been written.

My task was smoothed, as ever, by that coolly efficient and warmly human institution, the Auckland Institute and Museum library. Without the assistance of Ian Thwaites and his staff the book could not have been written or — thanks to assistant librarian Gordon Maitland — fully illustrated. It was also a pleasure to work with Mervyn Sterling, curator, Otamatea Kauri and Pioneer Museum, who freely made available museum resources, particularly the fine photographic collection which will receive justice when a definitive local history is written. Acknowledgement is also due to Anne Carpenter who coaxed clean images from old glass negatives and copied presentable photographs from indifferent originals. David and Sherry Reynolds, occasional Matakohe residents, suggested useful sources for enquiry. I am in debt to David for photographing the Ngati Whatua porch carving and the bust of Queen Victoria and to Sherry for unearthing the surprising pamphlet, *Naughty Doings at Port Albert.*

A particular debt is due to Matakohe resident Caryl Smith who gave her time and computer to the task of putting the book on disc. She cheerfully deciphered a sometimes patchy manuscript and her skills made it possible to meet a tight publishing deadline.

Before a book was contemplated, when Pahi was simply a place of retreat, I received a grounding in local history from two descendants of Albertlanders, Stella Fenwick, nee Hames, and Ralph Cliff, and from commercial fishermen Peter Yardley, John Fenwick and Brian Stubbs. To them I express gratitude. Subsequent discussions with my friends and occasional Pahi neighbours, Brian and Lindsay Corban, cast the die that turned my holiday house into a word factory. Whether I should feel gratitude for that, I'm not sure.

Finally, in probing into personal lives, I have been conscious of the validity of centenarian Robert Sterling's reply to one of my questions about his contemporary, Gordon Coates. Otherwise forthcoming, on this sensitive point he stiffened and said, "If I knew I wouldn't tell you." There is a proverb that declares we should speak well of the dead but is an historian as free, say, to discard people as some of the subjects of his enquiry have been? Dead victims have the right to be heard, too. Expatriate New Zealand writer, Dan Davin, recently addressed the question in his book *Closing Times*. Should epitaphs always be favourable? he asked. "It may be so for the truly dead. It is certainly a way of ensuring that they do not come alive. No man rises from an efficiently whited sepulchre." Well put, I think, almost as well as when over a hundred years ago, Henry Scotland said "praise indiscriminately showered. . .has become. . .an object of suspicion." The most considerable of Pahi residents, his life and work forgotten, Scotland wrote this in 1878 in a minor classic of radical thought *The New Zealander on London Bridge*. The quotation reads:

> The high-polite style has also been introduced into New Zealand. Unless prepared to praise up extravagantly any person or thing he may have occasion to speak or write about, a man in that colony will soon be given most unmistakably to understand that the sooner he holds his peace or withholds his pen the better for him. The same consequence has resulted. . .that praise, indiscriminately showered upon everything and everybody, has become almost worthless, and in most cases an object of suspicion.

—Dick Scott
Pahi and Auckland

Note to the third edition

The concluding passages of the original foreword, echoing Voltaire's 'We must respect the living but nothing but truth is good enough for the dead,' went unheeded in one response to the chapter on Gordon Coates — a family-commissioned biography that diluted the record of his extra-marital children. Coates himself had no such inhibitions: after having so many daughters, legitimate and otherwise, his part-Maori son was a source of pride. Visiting the public works camp where his son worked, Coates reportedly shouted 'Where's my boy?' as he opened the boot of his ministerial car to produce a keg of beer for the men. I am indebted to the Northland historian, the late Jack Lee, for advising me of this addendum to a chapter that reviewers found 'a sympathetic portrayal of a strangely ambivalent man.' *DS*

Bust of the young Queen Victoria and Union Jack presented by Governor Gore Browne to Ngati Whatua chiefs at Aotea (Shelly Beach) South Kaipara.

1. The fatal compact

English trees and shrubs are everywhere, following the example of the Pakeha who takes possession wherever he goes. . .and in time will probably do so to the exclusion of the 'sons of the soil'. . .But we must hasten. Who tolls the bell? Why who but Kitohi [Gittos] himself who is of course in his glory among his Maori children.
— The *Weekly News* visits Tanoa, 1885

William Gittos. . .gained a great influence over them, ultimately becoming their director in things temporal as well as spiritual.
-*Auckland Star* obituary, 1916

A concrete plinth standing before the Ngati Whatua meeting house opposite the "Cathedral of Gittos" at Tanoa is waiting for the return of a plaster and wood bust of the young Queen Victoria that Governor Gore Browne gave to the tribe as a reward for loyalty to the British during the wars for the land.[1] Until the royal head is set in place, aluminium frame windows are the only feature of this unusually bare wharenui set in an empty paddock.

This plain building was once the great house Aotearoa, host to Maori parliaments and the pride of a tribe that extended from Tamaki to Maunganui Bluff. It was adorned with the long sinuous sculpture in wood that is unique to the Ngati Whatua, but when the house was shifted by raft and bullock team from Shelly Beach, south Kaipara, to the mission village of Kakaraea (now Tanoa), it was stripped of its carvings. They were sold to buy Bibles.[2] The house has rested uneasily on its new site. There has been dispute as to which way it should face. Three times it has been jacked up and swung around on runners greased with cooking fat — a heavy task for muscle-power with a building 90 feet (72m) long and 30 feet (24m) wide. But then the tribe itself had been uprooted, hauled through history and pushed in conflicting directions.

Central figure during the first years of European settlement of the Kaipara, the thirty crucial years 1856-1886, was the Wesleyan missionary, William Gittos. A carpenter, "converted to God" at the age of seventeen, Gittos became a lay preacher three years later. He worked the Auckland circuit but showed little talent for preaching and after five years applied for "native work." As a family history remarks, his better educated wife Marianne "wrote many of his sermons. . .this aspect of his work sent no one into raptures. The chances are that his heart was less in the expounding of theology than in the practical side of mission work."[3]

On the Kaipara there was no call for mental tussles with non-believers. Christianity had been adopted a generation before through the work of Maori converts who had visited the first mission stations further north. As early as 1842 when the missionary, William Colenso, rowed up the Otamatea River he came upon the house of what he supposed to be "a respectable European." The owner was absent but the door was open and he found everything "very clean and tidy," well-equipped with kitchen utensils and comfortable furniture. "A mattress, bolster and pillow were rolled neatly together; a glazed and coloured print, representing the crucifixion of Christ, hung against the wall." He was astonished to discover later that this was the home of "William Stephenson, the Baptized Native Teacher." (William Stephenson — Wiremu Tipene — had been given the name of an English mission official, as was customary.)[4]

All around the Kaipara, Maori teachers had stolen a march on the missionaries. After slaughter to the point of genocide by Ngapuhi after the battle of Te Ikaaranganui in 1825 the demoralized Ngati Whatua were especially receptive to any message of security and hope. Five hundred Ngapuhi, most with muskets, led by Hongi Hika in chain-armour, had attacked a thousand Ngati Whatua warriors with two muskets between them. The Ngati Whatua fought desperately, absorbing musket volleys and then closing in with traditional weapons. It is said that 70 of the invaders were killed, including Hongi's son, but nearly all the defenders fell. Dead bodies floated with the tide down the Otamatea like shoals of mullet. The scale of the slaughter is comprehensible in terms of the fate of one Uriohau hapu: Pairama Mu has related that the only survivors in his extended family were his father, Patoro Mu, and four kinsman. The other 65 were killed.[5]

Those who retreated to the great hill-top pa on Pukehuia and other pa were mopped up in lesser battles and stragglers were hunted down as far as the Waikato. When William Gittos arrived in 1856, a generation later, the Kaipara was populated by only a remnant of a once great tribe. In a Maori census undertaken in 1866 by John Rogan, the land commissioner, there were found to be 269 men, 171 women, 88 boys and 71 girls in the whole of the Kaipara. Auckland Provincial Council returns for 1870 showed that, from Pouto to Pahi, the Uriohau (Ngati Whatua sub tribe) numbered 206. With this remnant Gittos quickly established a strong position. He could speak the language fluently (learned as a boy on the Hokianga) and only 26, he was powerfully built, intolerant, quick to anger, certain of his superiority: his first mission station on the Oruawharo River at Waingohi, near the future Port Albert, became not a spiritual centre but a command post. As a local historian puts it, "Gittos was more than a guide, philosopher and friend; he was builder and boatman. . .interpreter and diplomat. . .doctor and surgeon. . .financial adviser and unpaid trustee."[6] And even more again as *The Albertlanders* approvingly records: "His advice and word were law among the Oruawharo Maoris."

In establishing theocratic rule, Gittos was greatly helped by his experienced uncle, William White, in 1836 very likely the first European to sail into the harbour.[7] Formerly superintendent of Wesleyan missions, White had arrived in New Zealand in 1823. He had been expelled from the church for land-grabbing, timber dealing and too-fervent fellowship with his female converts. Ignoring a banishment order from New Zealand he remained in the timber trade, settled on the Kaipara, and as the years passed, was presented to Albertlander newcomers as "an associate minister" or "assistant to Rev Gittos," a deception that could not have pleased the Wesleyan church.

Organizing the purchase of Maori land was, from the first, a major part of Gittos's work. But unlike his uncle, he worked for the government and not himself — a gift of 100 acres accepted by his wife the only exception. The Ngati Whatua were as willing to sell land as they were to buy Christianity and even more the reason for this was the need for security from the Ngapuhi. The government's strategic plan, to place a cushion of European settlement between the Ngapuhi and Auckland coincided exactly with the Ngati Whatua desire to have a buffer zone of Pakeha settlement between them and the north. Gittos assumed the role of facilitator. *The Albertlanders* goes so far as to give him credit, "not generally understood," for masterminding both "genesis and development" of the Albertland settlement for reasons of defence. The implication of this policy, that the worthy lower middle class Albertlanders, the antithesis of military settlers, were simply musket fodder should the Ngapuhi raid south, is not pursued.

Land sales from sea to sea began in earnest the year Gittos arrived. The signatures William Gittos, Wesleyan Missionary, William White, Merchant, Kaipara, appeared as joint witnesses on early documents. In October 1856, using Tokatoka peak for a trig station, Te Kopuru stream as northern boundary, a 12,000 acre (4.500 hectare) block from the Tasman Sea to the Northern Wairoa was sold for £350. For this important first step, Donald McLean, Chief Land Commissioner, signed on behalf of the government. Eager as they were to surrender the land, Paikea Te Hekeua, Manukau Rewarewa and 27 other

Tanoa, "Paikea's village on the Otamatea", from surveyor S. Percy Smith's sketchbook, 1860.

PAPAROA
continued.

Boundaries.
[15,021 acres.]

tonu atu. A hei tohu mo to matou whakaaetanga ki nga tikanga katoa o tenei Puka-puka kua tuhituhia nei o matou ingoa me o matou tohu. A hei tohu hoki mo te whaka-aetanga o te Kuini o Ingarani mo tana wahi ki nga tikanga katoa o tenei Pukapuka kua tuhia nei te ingoa o John Rogan D.C. Kaiwhakarite Whenua. Ko nga rohe enei o taua whenua ka timata i Oruatara kei te wai o Paparoa—ka haere i runga o te rohe o Mata-kohe ki Te Ngutukaikiwi, Otara, Matakohe, Poauau ka tae ki Waitaeore, ka ahu whaka te Marangai 251°. 0'. 133.—32 riki—296°. 0'. 460 riki—251°. 0'. 253.—70 riki ka whiti Te Angeange 220. 39. 234 riki—276°. 54'. 6243 riki, ka tae ki Otupua ka haere whaka te tonga 358°. 50'.—20600 riki ka whiti wai kopikopiko, Pakaraka 24°. 33.'—15600 riki ka whiti whakatakatewai ka tae ki te Pahi—ka haere i te takutai o te wai o te Pahi ki te kongutuawa o Whakatakatewai, Pohutu, Motu Nga pewa Tai karekare, Whakaruku, Aute, Te Makaka Waiangarara, Omarae, Te Rangeora, ka haere i te takutai o te wai o Paparoa Waipao, Kauriwakaporo, Tapuaeharuru, Heremata, a Oruatara ka tutuki te rohe kei reira.

Tutaemakanoa
Reserve.
[78 acres.]

Kotahi te wahi e mahue ki a matou i roto o tenei whenua ko Tutaemakanoa kua oti te ruri, ko nga eka o taua wahi 78a. 0r. 0p. kua oti hoki te whakahua ki te taha o tenei pukapuka.

Arama Karaka.
The mark x of Puriri.
manukau.
The mark x of Poihipi.
The mark x of Maka.
The mark x of Matenga.
Wiremu Tipene x.
Matikikuha x.
The mark x of Makoare.
na te Manihera x.
The mark x of Matiu.
The mark x of Paratene.
Matini.
The mark x of Heremaia.
Wiremu Apo.
Awaiti.
pairama.
hirini.
henare.
The mark x of te Kepa.
The mark x of Pua.
The mark x of te Tana.
The mark x of Reihana.
The mark x of Rangina.
The mark x of Arama.
The mark x of Taniora.
The mark x of Heta.
The mark x of Kamaima.
The mark x of Te toka.
The mark x of Kaiwaka.
The mark x of Puekara.
The mark x of Kare.
The mark x of Hemana.
The mark x of Netana.
The mark x of Waitoetoe.

mi haka Karena.
Hamahona.
Honewata.
Hemi.
te turi.
te ahimawiti.
The mark x of Tamati Tara.
The mark x of Pita.
The mark x of Hona.
The mark x of Nikora.
The mark x of Himiona.
The mark x of Tame.
The mark x of Horitanga.
The mark x of Hori Keha.
The mark x of Paramena.
The mark x of Paramena.
The mark x of Piripi.
pai rama te hira.
The mark x of Piripi.
The mark x of Iraia.
The mark x of Hone Kingi.
The mark x of Pereniki.
The mark x of Patara.
The mark x of Te Awe.
Hone Waite.
The mark x of Waikapa.
The mark x of Rupua.
The mark x of Tamehana.
The mark x of Paraone.
The mark x of Paki.
eramiha.
The mark x of Te Poari.
timoti.
The mark x of Ihaia.
The mark x of Hakopa.

The mark x of Pihama.
The mark x of Tiraha.
The mark x of te Whenga.
The mark x of Tipene Makoare.
The mark x of Hami.
The mark x of Kumera.
The mark x of Nikora.
The mark x of Nauihi.
The mark x of Tamati Hemana.
The mark x of Paratene Do.
The mark x of Wikirepe.
The mark x of Tatana.
The mark x of Hemitipene.
The mark x of Paikea.

Boys {
The mark x of Paikea Ewarewha.
The mark x of Taranui.
The mark x of Were-weti.
}

The mark x of Henare Potaia.
The mark x of Tuarua Hori.
The mark x of Hohua.
The mark x of Te Kiri Painga.
The mark x of Neba pihama.
The mark x of Riki.
The mark x of Hone Piki.
The mark x of Paemona ika nui.
The mark x of Tioriori.
The mark x of Horomona.
The mark x of Matiu tutura.
The mark x of Hone hihi.
The mark x of Kerepe.
The mark x of Miriama.

The mark of Taraipene.

Ko nga tangata i kite i te hoatutanga o nga moni me te tuhinga o nga ingoa—
Keene. Paraone. Tamati.

Signatories to sale of Pahi-Paparoa block, 1858 (from Turton's copy of the original, 1878).

signatories still lamented their action. An official document is an unlikely place to find poignant feelings but the deed of sale expresses their sorrow:

> We have entirely given up and wept over and bidden farewell to this land inherited from our forefathers with its rivers its lakes its streams its spring its timber its stones and its grass with its plains its forests its fertile spots and its barren places and all and everything above the surface of the said Land or beneath the surface of the said Land and all and everything connected with the said Land we have now for ever delivered up to the Queen of England. . .[8]

Land sales had also begun from the Pacific Coast. By 1858 it was only a question of mopping up the interior. That year Pahi peninsula and its Paparoa hinterland, a block of 15,021 acres, were sold for 8d an acre. The chiefs Arama Karaka (Adam Clark), Manukau and Paikea signed their names, as did Hone Waite (John White) and Wiremu Tipene, the mission teachers. Man and boy the Uriohau signed or placed their mark — 102 signatures in all — on a document that left no doubt as to its binding nature:

> The Deed written on this Twentythird (23) day of December in the Year of our Lord 1858 is a full and final sale conveyance and surrender by us the Chiefs and People of the Tribe of Te Uriohau whose names are hereunto subscribed. And Witnesseth that on behalf of ourselves, our relatives and descendants we have by signing this Deed under the shining sun of this day parted with and forever transferred unto Victoria Queen of England. . .in consideration of the Sum of five hundred Pounds fourteen shillings (£500.14). . .all that piece of our land situated at Kaipara (Arapaoa) and named Paparoa. . .with its trees minerals waters rivers lakes streams and all appertaining to the said land and all our right title claim and interest whatsoever thereon To Hold to Queen Victoria Her Heirs and Assigns as a lasting possession absolutely for ever and ever.[9]

On the Pahi peninsula, burial places among the limestone outcrops above Tokatapu, the sacred rock, and a network of cleverly fortified pa sites were included in the deal. No longer were there references to weeping and bidding farewell to the land: its sale had become a routine transaction. By the following year a quarter of a million acres had been sold for £9,151, an average of 9d an

Paikea Te Hekeua

acre. Almost as much again was being surveyed for sale or was under offer. A broad belt reaching across Northland from the Tasman to the Pacific was available for Pakeha settlement: the strategic buffer was in place. Wildly enthusiastic endorsements of an Albertland association to promote migration of nonconformists to New Zealand gave promise that it would be populated.

In 1862, bi-centenary year of the expulsion of nonconforming ministers from the Church of England, the first two Albertland ships brought 1000 passengers to Auckland. Learning the truth about their 40-acre grants — their isolation, their worthlessness — about half the migrants elected to stay in Auckland. And only a small proportion of the 2000 who followed in the next four ships made the doubtful journey north. In all, fewer than 300 finally settled on the "free" land they had paid good passage money to claim. William Gittos was at Port Albert to encourage the optimistic ones and a Maori feast was arranged at Tanoa. Those Paparoa-bound were provided with his boat (and willing Maori oarsmen) and feasted by Manukau at Karakanui before landing at Pahi. Maori supplies of kumara, fish and fruit rescued early families from starvation. "Many a lost and weary traveller was guided by them to safety and comfort," records *The Albertlanders*. "In sickness, accidents and similar troubles they were always ready to tender every possible aid."

The land wars were simmering in Taranaki and Waikato at this time and in July 1863 the Royal Irish were ambushed near present day Bombay Hill and there were other fatal skirmishes even closer to Auckland. Dr James Bell, the Albertland medical officer, who had been invited to a korero of Kaipara chiefs at Tanoa, reported to the settlers:

> They were cognizant to a surprising degree of all that was going on in different parts of the island; they named facts of a later date than the settlers were in receipt of by post. They were of the opinion. . . that tribes in the north might think of taking England at a disadvantage in the present state of affairs, join the rebels, or start a new feud on their own account. . .Paikia [sic] and those with him would defend us in a case of necessity, a blow struck at a Pakeha in Kaipara would be struck at him. . .They would be prepared for anything; and if necessary to flee in the event of the worst, he would. . .expedite our transit to a place of safety. He would collect the Paparoa and Matakohe settlers and bring them to Port Albert. . .At present the Maoris recommend no more active measure than a supply of arms.[10]

No Ngapuhi crossed the buffer zone but the following year some 200 Waikato prisoners taken at Rangiriri were confined on Kawau Island. In 1864 they escaped, broke into groups, and set up camp around the Kaipara. Gittos, who was visiting Auckland, urgently returned via Manukau Harbour to dampen any local sympathy they might arouse. His ship was met by heavy seas on Kaipara bar and after tacking for several hours, the captain decided to turn back. Gittos took the wheel, ordered sails trimmed, and to the screams of passengers rode the first huge breaker, touched bottom with a grinding bump, and went in with the next wave. Susanna Cullen, Maungaturoto-bound, has left on record that when the captain resumed control of the wheel "he was as white as chalk."[11] An impressive performance. And with their "father" on hand, the Gittos flock rejected the escaped prisoners "in spite of all arguments and entreaties." In the words of one Waikato, "They listened and turned away their faces." The response was hardly

Arama Karaka
(Adam Clark)

in doubt since a deserter from the British forces invading the Waikato, given provisions by a Port Albert settler and sent further north for safety, had to flee back in the night before the Ngati Whatua turned him in.[12]

By now Gittos had sorted out Arama Karaka as his lieutenant. Paikea, Karaka's Otamatea neighbour, was ailing and growing old, Manukau, up river at Karakanui, tended to be unsound on the liquor question and was not always co-operative when land prices were being fixed.[13] In 1886, Gittos moved the mission from the Oruawharo to the Otamatea River, siting it near Karaka's Tanoa village but in privacy at Rangiora on the opposite shore. From his office window he could see smoke curling up from the cooking fires.

The mission house was large and built from the very best of heart kauri by Pakeha tradesmen. With its sturdy timbers, high ceilings and generous verandahs it is still impressive.[14] Several Pakeha servants and abundant Maori labour ensured that Gittos lived comfortably. The mission had ample funds given freely by the people as he arranged the continued sale and lease of their lands and timber. Arama Karaka himself received a government retainer for facilitating the sales. Other chiefs and mission teachers were also on the payroll.

Retaining their independence, the king movement tribes to the south had dominated coastal shipping before the land wars and their crops and flour mills had kept Auckland in food. The Ngati Whatua elected to live on their capital. And with enormous tracts to sell even a few pence per acre brought large sums for a small population. Enough for the tribe to dress in the height of fashion, own the fastest racehorses, the best yachts and generally eat, drink and be merry. Joseph Masefield, trading from a bark hut at Oahau (now Batley) since the early sixties, built a large store and hotel to meet a demand that regularly emptied his shelves. In spectacular reversal of usual colonial roles, the "white man" slogged and sometimes near-starved in the bush while "the natives" lolled about the beach sipping rum.

The Kaipara had been one of the great Maori waterways. It had been alive with canoes — fishing, trading, ferrying passengers and moving freight. Big sailing canoes had plied its waters (twin sailed craft were used in European times) and a name for the Kaipara entrance, Tahuri waka whakarere wahine, so many widows from drowning, (literally from overturned canoes), speaks of how far they ventured. The harbour was a fish bowl. The first Pakeha settlers spoke of the din made by snapper crunching shellfish and they caught snapper in bulk for dog food. The surveyor, S. Percy Smith, wrote in his 1860 journal, "The harbour is celebrated for its fish. Among these are mullet or kanae, a jumping fish which are usually caught by pulling a canoe along the mud banks at the time the tide is rising and the moon in the right quarter, when the fish, in trying to escape as the canoe comes along, jump into the canoe."[15]

Maori recruits were not accepted into the British Navy but Maori knowledge of the harbour was so detailed that when HMS *Pandora* surveyed the Kaipara in 1852 the commander turned a blind eye to regulations and put Piri Waata of Aratapu into uniform with petty officer rank. His services as a pilot were so satisfactory that he stayed on the ship for the rest of its voyage around New Zealand.[16] Arama Karaka's mission village made one effort to draw on such traditional skills by buying an expensive trading cutter but it was beached before long and Gittos leased it to a Pakeha. The fate of the tribe's seafaring traditions was written in the fate of Taheretikitiki " the warrior's crest," most

The great Kaipara war canoe, Taheretikitiki, on the Waitemata. It was 84 feet (25.6m) long, 5 feet (1.5m) wide amidships and its 50 paddlers defeated two 12-oared cutters from HMS *Tauranga* over a hard fought two-mile course.

famous of Kaipara war canoes. Built of kauri for the ceremonial use of Ngati Whatua chief, Paora Tuhaere of Orakei, it raced to victory against all comers on Waitemata Harbour and was later used by King Tawhiao to ferry distinguished visitors across the Waikato. The canoe was floated on an artificial lake at the 1906 Christchurch Exhibition and then left to the mercy of vandals in Hagley Park. Restored by the government for the American fleet's visit in 1908, it was again neglected and only the prow was saved for Auckland Museum.* One porch carving from the Aotearoa house that found its way to Rotorua Museum and one carved lintel in the British Museum[17] are two other relics of Uriohau culture that survived handling by the "curio dealer" customers of the mission.

The price in loss of Maori values was heavy, but with carvings rejected as graven images, women forbidden the moko, children memorising names of English kings, Gittos was not yet satisfied. Scattered about the Kaipara were pockets of land reserved from sale because they were the sacred places of the ancestors. Their total area was small. Measured against the vast tracts sold, it was minuscule. Not their size but their abiding spiritual power bothered him.

In all the 15,000-acre Paparoa block one 78-acre piece had been held in Maori ownership. The land was on the west bank of Pahi River, just before the headwaters narrowed and the river began twisting and looping back on itself. It was behind a mangrove-filled bay and below a high pa-topped ridge that gushed fresh-water springs from its base — one of the few permanent supplies on the whole peninsula.

---

* Taheretikitiki's most recent appearance was on the covers of *Looking Backward*, a 1980 pictorial history by Sinclair and Harrex. It was described as "the famous Waikato carved canoe" — another humiliation if the Maori were always to take Pakeha historians seriously.

On the Waikato, 1904. Tufts of albatross feathers form warrior plumage (hihi) on the carved prow.

Placenames indicate that this was a site where the most profound rites had been enacted in pre-Christian times. The reserve was named Tutaimakanoa (throwing excrement at random) and the bay it fronted on was called Whakaruku (submit to ceremonial washing). Around the next bluff, past the narrow passage guarded by Tokatapu was Taikarekare (beam of a privy).[18] The river has a powerful presence in these upper reaches, almost an eerie quality (remarked by those without knowledge of its history) and here, it seems, the tapu of the earth was lifted by religious rituals that purged the individual of his profane origins. This was accomplished by biting the beam of a latrine and then being immersed in water. Tane's ascent through the heavens to receive baskets of occult knowledge required that he be purified in this manner before entering the tenth heaven.[19] The spiritual significance of this place had to be expunged. Gittos arranged its sale to a Pakeha farmer.

At least this was semi-remote ancestral territory. Gittos also focused on the shades of the parents and grandparents of the living. Present-day Whakapirau was shown on early maps as Wahi Tapu, a religious place, because the remains of recent battle victims lay there. How the presence of the dead was neutralized by building a mausoleum — and the sequel — is described in later chapters.

For Arama Karaka who had abandoned his father's name, Haututu, to take the name Adam Clark, psychological remaking was complete with rejection of the tapu that surrounded his father's death. Haututu had been killed defending his land from Ngapuhi muskets in 1825. His body had been taken by canoe down the Otamatea to be cooked and eaten at his own Kakaraea kainga. A big pohutukawa marked this especially tapu ground. The missionary set out to destroy the tapu by employing Europeans to build a church on the site. A handsome building with great kauri beams supporting a high vaulted roof, it became known as the "Cathedral Church of Gittos." At first Arama Karaka was afraid to enter it and violate his father's memory but Gittos persuaded him with a prayer. The church was opened in March 1877 and in April "a great native meeting" was held at Kakaraea. Two resolutions set the seal on abject surrender to the wishes of William Gittos. They were:

> That the tribe entrusts all their troubles and difficulties to the European members of the district, instead of the Maori members, to bring such matters before parliament;
> The name that this, the Ngati Whatua tribe shall be for the future known by, as a mark of loyalty and obedience to the laws of God and the Queen, is The Englishmen.[20]

Arama Karaka confirmed the serious intent of these decisions at the anniversary celebrations attended by some 200 Maoris the following year. "It was pretty well known now all over New Zealand he was no longer a Maori but a Pakeha," he said. And the chief Pairama added that "now all the Maoris had become Pakehas" then by intermarriage "they should become one indeed." A recently arrived land speculator, "Captain" Colbeck JP, took the chair, and the guest speaker, a visiting parson, "compared the aboriginals of Australia to the Maoris, in which the 'black fellows' came off second best." Gittos preached at both morning and evening services, he introduced speakers, offered up prayers, led Maori children singing Moody and Sankey hymns, pronounced the

Ngati Whatua porch panel.

The "Cathedral Church of Gittos" built at Kakaraea (Tanoa) in 1877. Lionel de Labrosse was one of the builders.

benediction. As the *Daily Southern Cross* admiringly put it, "Mr Gittos was ubiquitous."[21]

Arama Karaka was a familiar figure as he accompanied his mentor around the harbour. He often spoke at church services and Gittos translated. He was obese, and for the irreverent, the miracle that caught attention was how his horse managed to carry him. An English observer has left a lukewarm appraisal; "He is a very tall and very portly personage. He is a great man, corporeally certainly, and perhaps in other ways as well. . .Arama rules his little community in paternal and patriarchal spirit. . .and in most things accepts the guidance of his friend the missionary."[22]

Another writer has recorded how patriarchs rule. Some young men who had been drinking were made to walk in a circle while Karaka "laid on a lancewood with all his strength until he was tired. Prohibition enforced with such vigour was effective."[23] It was an action worthy of the missionary who had once put an axe through a chief's keg of liquor. "If it was not you, Kitohi, but any other man, he would be dead!" was the outraged — yet conciliatory — reply.

In his own home Gittos ruled no differently. He is remembered as "autocratic, paternalistic and inflexible." A family history relates that "William would invite people into the house without notice. . . Marianne would be obliged to dash into the fowlyard and wring the neck of the first chicken she could catch. She was very deaf and her children considered she had a very hard life." Marianne Gittos was a skilled apiarist — the first in New Zealand to use the improved frame that made commercial beekeeping possible. Her husband did not share her skill:

> She could handle them without any form of protection, moving them aside with a feather. Not so William. Returning home on horseback one day. . .Marianne asked him to stop at the hive and bring some honey. Both rider and horse were sweaty and presumably the smell upset the bees which immediately launched a mass attack upon William. He escaped only by jumping into the well. One suspects that the children treasured this story with some relish.[24]

The extra-legal punishment Gittos caused to be inflicted on a well-connected young Pakeha who courted his daughter Esther — an incident that slipped past the family historian — speaks loudest of the power and personality of the man who dominated all those around him for so long. Young Frederick Fairburn met Esther Gittos when working for his father Edwin Fairburn, government surveyor, during the Great North Road survey from Auckland to Whangarei. He must have taken side-trips to the Kaipara mission station on his days off. Aged 21, he was well-spoken, well-educated and musical. He had spent several years in Europe holidaying with his family on the proceeds of the sale of land acquired by his grandfather, William Fairburn, a lay preacher with Samuel Marsden's first mission station at the Bay of Islands. Fred Fairburn became engaged to Esther Gittos but she was not quite of age and her father ordered him from the house and gave instructions that he be horse-whipped should he return.

After Esther reached marriageable age Fairburn wrote to announce that he would be revisiting the family and duly presented himself one Sunday evening when Gittos was absent. He was savagely assaulted, arrested next day for "being on the premises of the Rev William Gittos for an unlawful purpose" and taken before three Port Albert justices of the peace who held him without bail pending a supreme court hearing. The case was given wide-spread publicity "not only on account of the nature of the charge but of the social position of the parties." Some excerpts from the deposition hearing:

> Mrs Gittos deposed she. . .saw Fairburn at the door. He put up his hand to silence her. He said he just wanted five minutes. She said 'no five minutes' and ordered him off. Her eldest daughter. . .called on him to go out. On his refusal she struck him and called for help. The manservant was there in an instant, collared him by the throat and threw him on his back, and held him while her second daughter got a horsewhip, which she used about him. . . . During this time herself and two daughters used the horsewhip on Fairburn. . .. After several minutes the servant man released him on his promise to go. After a pause he rushed through the casement, breaking a pane of glass in leaving.

Sarah Gittos corroborated her mother's evidence:

> When she saw prisoner Fairburn she exclaimed, 'What! are you here?' He held up his hand for her to be quiet, tried to put her out of the room. She hit him in the face with her fist and called for help. Sam Atkinson was quickly there, and threw Fairburn on the floor. . . . Her sister fetched a riding whip and used it vigorously on Fairburn. Her mother then took it and used it freely on him. He yelled with his might and said, 'My God, there is houseful of fiends!'. . . Sam was giving Fairburn a good hammering. Witness went for a rope to tie him up, but Mrs Gittos said 'let him go; it will be better he should be away before Mr Gittos returns.' She then took the whip and used it about him. She told Sam to thrash him off the place.[25]

Three women had flogged Fairburn as he lay, face up, immobilized in a

Marianne and William Gittos, their seven children and a grandchild. Esther is sitting next to her father, Sarah next to her mother. Back row: John, Clare, Kathleen, Marion and Eric.

stranglehold by the servant. The sisters had also joined Atkinson in punching his upturned face — a busy end to a sabbath day of rest down at the mission. What more would Gittos have done? And the unwanted suitor? Perhaps he was truly besotted by Esther's charms. While whipping him in the garden as he tried to escape, Atkinson fell in a ditch and Fairburn managed to gain possession of the whip. Miss Gittos demanded that he give it to her. He meekly complied. Essie, as she had been affectionately known in friendlier circumstances, handed it back to the servant.

Gittos gave evidence that when he returned home local Maoris were waiting for him to give orders to "capture" Fairburn. He told them the Port Albert policeman would be doing that. He said that his daughter had immediately broken off the engagement when he told her that Fairburn was involved with

23

Hangi for a Kaipara wedding photographed by George Gallie. Note who peels the kumara.

two other young women in the few months he had been waiting for her birthday.

> I made inquiries as to Fairburn's character, the result being I found him to be the meanest and basest man I had ever thought, heard, or read about. *By Fairburn:* Will you state your authority? *Mr Gittos:* I had better refer you to the young woman you ruined in Auckland. *By the Bench:* Is that answer satisfactory? *Fairburn:* Yes. *Mr Gittos:* The prisoner was also engaged to another young lady in Auckland. . .[26]

Gittos said that he had destroyed letters Fairburn had written to him "as being unfit for perusal." Two were put in as evidence, however. They were not read in court and the press was refused access to them. Later it emerged that one had threatened to "divulge and publish family secrets of a nature not obscurely hinted at" if Gittos continued to deny access to his daughter. And the other, written after his arrest, had "more explicitly rehearsed the infamous charge against the honour of the lady for whom he still avowed an undying love."

Fairburn was committed for trial in the supreme court and held without bail. One newspaper noted that before reaching its verdict the bench recalled Gittos "and held a private conversation. . .not audible in court, much to the surprise of the persons present." His control of proceedings was so blatant that Thomas Gubb, a prominent Albertlander orchardist (and later Rodney county chairman)

24

was moved to write to the paper reporting that Gittos had been in collusion with the bench before the hearing as well as after it.

> Imagine my surprise at seeing three JPs and the prosecutor sitting around a table in conversation relating to the case, and the constable joined the group. . . .While this was going on where was the prisoner? In the lock-up. At least twenty minutes must have passed in this manner.[27]

Gubb spoke of the justices' "strange and seemingly partial conduct" and protested at their refusal to grant bail. They replied that the case had gone from 10am to 6pm and so there was no time to consider bail. Gubb wrote again to dismiss this "quibble." As the supreme court session in Auckland was three months away their refusal "amounted to three months imprisonment for the prisoner." Meanwhile an Auckland magistrate intervened and set Fairburn free pending his trial.

The Gittos writ did not extend beyond the Kaipara. When the case reached the high court, Mr Justice Gillies was scathing in his address to the grand jury. Frederick Fairburn, he said, was

> . . .committed for being illegally on premises. . . .I must tell you that such a charge is not an indictable offence. There is no such offence. . . The circumstances are peculiar. The young man charged was enamoured of a young lady and was forbidden in the house. But he persisted in coming there. He is found, one evening, on the premises. There is no evidence of his going there for any felonious purpose. . .you will be bound to throw out the bill as containing no offence known to the law.[28]

Frederick Fairburn's family suggested that he should spend time in Australia until the scandal died down. He found his way to Perth where he became a

Constable Jonas Abrams, en route to Pahi Courthouse.

professor of music.[29] He never returned and lost contact with the land of his birth — except, perhaps, for the philandering genes he bequeathed to his nephew, the poet A.R.D. Fairburn. His wronged fiancee, Esther Gittos, never married. Nor did her sister Marion. Three Gittos daughters did, including whip-wielding Sarah and Kathleen, a lady rifle-shot champion of New Zealand.

After riding high for a quarter-century William Gittos had suffered a severe rebuff. Less publicly, his tight theocratic domain was already coming apart. The settlers were left increasingly dissatisfied — indeed, bored — by his sermons. And more, they were challenging his autocratic ways. In one locally famous incident, a collection for Wesleyan missions was sent to Gittos from Maungaturoto. He sent it back saying that handling such money was the work of his treasurer. It was "felt that Mr Gittos could have quite easily passed the money on to the treasurer so they gave it back to those who donated it."[30] As Pakeha contributions dwindled, Gittos complained, in a phrase that has gone into folklore, "There is only one half crown in Otamatea County — and no-one knows who has it."

More importantly, the endless supply of Maori money and Maori muscle was also drying up. A new generation was becoming disenchanted. While remaining loyal to the Queen, says *The History of Methodism,* many younger men were becoming indifferent to the gospel. "In the early days, the older men would act as boats' crew for the love of the gospel — conducting their missionary on long journeys asking only for their food. Later, the younger Maoris demanded payment, often exorbitant payment, for their services."

Gittos was forced to row himself. "Up and down the long reaches. . .he would sail or row his boat. Obliged to work the tides for many years he did as much travel by night as by day. Through rain or fog. . .he was always on the job. Only a strong man both mentally and physically could have done it but eventually. . .he was a martyr to rheumatism."

In 1886, at the age of 56, Gittos gave up the mission. He visited Taranaki that year with hopes of influencing the Parihaka chief, Te Whiti-o-Rongomai, who had resumed passive resistance after release from exile. Received at Te Whiti's table, Gittos presumed to say grace uninvited. He was swiftly corrected. "Don't thank God for the food," said Te Whiti, "if you are going to thank anyone, thank me."[31] Away from the Englishmen tribe, it appeared, life would not be the same again.

William Gittos became Superintendent of Maori Missions, responsible for Methodist work in Northland, Waikato and the King Country. But neither broader horizons nor age mellowed him. As the family history sadly notes,

Ngati Whatua lintel (British Museum).

"More than one attempt was made to have him train a successor, but all attempts ended in conflict simply because William could not accept that changes had occurred. With age a little of the 'benevolence' had deserted the 'benevolent dictator.'" He retired in 1913 and died three years later at the age of eighty-six.

Many attempts had been made at Wesleyan conferences to persuade Gittos to record his thirty years of mission work on the Kaipara. After his death it was found that he had written nothing and destroyed all his papers. And worse, the journal of his uncle, William White, returned from England by a relative, had been mutilated. The pages covering the crucial years of activities that had led to his expulsion from the church had been cut out.

From the settlers' point of view, Gittos had served them well. To commemorate the 50th anniversary of the Albertlanders' arrival, a church at Wharehine, near Port Albert, was dedicated as the Gittos Memorial Church. From the Maori perspective such gains as he had brought had cost them dearly. Perhaps nothing could have saved the land, but did they have to lose their identity as well? Not long after his death the Englishmen tribe voted with its feet a non-memorial — it crossed over en masse to join the church of Tahupotiki Wiremu Ratana. Otamatea farmer Paraire Karaka Paikea, for ten years an ordained Methodist minister, joined his people in the exodus. His name appeared in the first list of apostles when the church was registered in 1925 and three years later he became the private secretary of Ratana himself. Chosen to represent one of the "Four Quarters," the North, Paikea stood as a Ratana candidate at three general elections and then in 1938 was elected to parliament under a Ratana-Labour banner and became a cabinet minister. Recognised as one of the most able of Ratana leaders, his seat was passed to his son, Tapihana, when he died in 1943.[32] In the churchyard of the "Cathedral of Gittos" the Paikea family tombstones and those around them bear the symbol Te Whetu Marama, the five pointed star and crescent moon that represents "the shining light" of Ratana's mission.

But the Gittos legacy is not dead. Henare Toka, the celebrated Ngati Whatua carver who had lived with his family at isolated Kapua Point, once came with his tools to restore carvings to Aotearoa, the meeting house at Tanoa. He had worked to adorn 38 houses of other tribes: his great wish before he died was to send chips flying for one of his own. He went away disappointed.[33] Money has been found for aluminium windows, not "heathen images." With a centenary of the re-siting of the house planned for November 1987 it is Queen Victoria's head and not the taonga of the tribe that it is hoped will be returned.

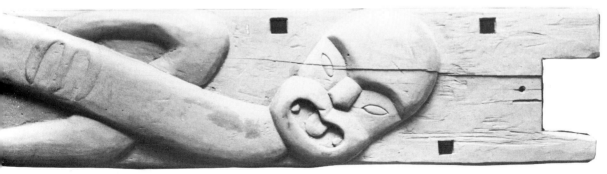

Detail from porch panel.

Sir Graham Latimer, leader of work that began in 1982 in preparation for the centenary, is of far north origins, but he embraces traditions from the era of the Englishmen tribe." The beginnings of modern society were layed down here," he says, "the first cemetery in the country where Maori and Pakeha were buried together is across the road. Ngati Whatua didn't want to come into Maoridom — you can see a marble handshake on one of the tombstones and that is the symbol of their wish to work hand-in-hand with the Pakeha."[34]

Sir Graham cites biblical texts to show that carvings are "against Christianity." He is opposed to their return and is anxious to see the bust of Queen Victoria placed on the waiting plinth. Mrs Susie Paikea, veteran of the first Ratana Lady Orchestra's visit to England and the last kuia resident at Tanoa, opposed the modernisation plans with such vehemence before she died that police were called to the marae. It is testimony to the great mana of the house that dispute should continue.

The "Cathedral" decapitated — for "safety reasons". The mellow churchyard has recently been "tidied" with a chainsaw.

2. Schemes and dreams

This week I came across a gold discovery — a specimen found which gave
1040oz to the ton — a fabulous return. Nothing is strange in this country,
always something new, and nothing a novelty.
-George Alderton on Colbeck's Kaipara settlement,
English *Agricultural Gazette*, 1879

In all the long history of Aotearoa did anyone have more brass than Captain
William Henry Colbeck? A successful Yorkshireman grown rich in the wool trade,
Colbeck came to New Zealand with his fortune in 1876 when he was 47 years
old. With the help of two sons he cut a swathe across the Kaipara that left open-
mouthed 40-acre settlers and 1000-acre landed gentry alike. He acquired a great
belt of land from the Pahi River to the Otamatea — 18,000 acres of freehold —
surveyed townships, established industries, took over a steam shipping line and
had himself elected to parliament — all in the first three years.

Colbeck's grand strategy was to reap a second fortune by transplanting to the
Kaipara many hundreds of families from Yorkshire and Lancashire under a
government "special settlement" scheme that reimbursed to the entrepreneur much
of the cost of his operations. It was land speculation on a stupendous scale.

Three towns were placed on the map and at one, Batley, named after his
Yorkshire home town, wharf, fish cannery, flour mill, general store and hotel
were built and town lots were sold at between £55 and £100 — prices that rivalled
Auckland's. At the second town, on Whakapirau creek, sections were snapped up
by absentee speculators before two boards could be nailed together and at the
third, Karaka, scene of inter-tribal slaughter, "he got rid of the tapu" by building
a mausoleum for the scattered bones and subdivided what has become modern
Whakapirau.[1]

Colbeck's confidence was displayed by the scale of the on-site headquarters
he built for himself. He took over the superbly placed property (with private
chapel) occupied at the head of Pahi River by the French count Lionel de
Labrosse and expanded it to make virtually a fourth village. His house,
reported in early 1878 to be "an extensive mansion, the total cost. . .into
thousands and. . .superior to any residence north of Auckland," was set in
formal gardens with 4-acre orchard attached. Living quarters, butchery,
cookhouse and store for between 20 and 30 farm workers and later for as many
contract bushmen, were provided nearby.[2] Even a racecourse was laid out for
their entertainment. Colbeck's title of "Captain" might be spurious — he had

simply served in the West Yorkshire Yeomanry Volunteers — but there was nothing bogus about his bank account.

Migration prospects on Colbeck's special settlement could not have been rosier if George Alderton, editor of the *Northern Advocate*, was to be believed. He planted this bait in the English *Agricultural Gazette* in 1879:

> My friend Captain Colbeck, has since his arrival here got about 1000 acres of land into grass, which carries 800 sheep, thirty dairy cows, about fifty fat cattle, besides young stock and horses; and 30 acres in crop, principally maize and oats. His residence is built on a very romantic spot, with a sheet of water in front (having the appearance of a lake), and a river at the back bending its serpentine course through a pretty undulating country. Every kind of fruit grows here most luxuriantly including oranges, bananas and melons; tobacco, rice, tea, sugar, olive, &c.,also grow here.
>
> I was over at Capt. Colbeck's residence this week; he is at present at Wellington representing this district in parliament, but I found his eldest son John lolling on the verandah discussing a cigar with a Mr Hopkins, of Berkshire. Both were at Oxford together, and were talking old times over. 'Varsity men and public school boys are as thick as peas in this part of the country; we can raise a cricket or football team of them at any time. So your readers will observe that our social status ought to be endurable. . .[3]

At the New Zealand end Alderton, who emerged as Colbeck's land agent in January 1880, tailored his pitch to an audience that knew all about tropical fruits and tropical crops luxuriating in the north. For them he settled for wheat at sixty bushells to the acre:

FARMS.   FARMS.   FARMS.

ON DEFERRED PAYMENT.

A SPECIAL SETTLEMENT FOR COLONISTS.

10,000 ACRES OF THE VERY BEST QUALITY OF LAND.

To be sold in lots to suit purchasers, on deferred payment (without residential or improvement conditions) being a portion of Captain W. H. Colbeck's Celebrated Kaipara Limestone Land.

So many applications having been made to Captain Colbeck, M.P., by persons residing in the Colony, to sell portions of his Kaipara Estate for Farms, he has decided to set apart about 10,000 acres for that purpose, and instructed the undersigned to dispose of the same before leaving for England, where it has been arranged to dispose of the remainder. Applications for the said 10,0.0 acres must be sent in to the undersigned immediately.

TERMS.—Cash or deferred payments. The most liberal that can be obtained anywhere. INQUIRE.

QUALITY.—It is the best description of land—limestone. It is easily got into grass; nothing but fern and tea-tree to deal with.

RESULTs.—Sixty bushels of wheat to the acre, without manure. Steam Flour-mill on block.

ACCESSIBILITY.—Bi-weekly steam communication with Auckland, weekly steam communication with the Northern Wairoa, where there is a population (at the mills) of about 2000 (consumers of settlers' produce.

PROSPECTs.—The Northern Railway, which is now being surveyed, passes near the block, and the land which is offered at a nominal figure, will in a few years be enhanced to at least ten times its present selling price.

APPLICANTS.—Full particulars can be obtained by a personal interview with the undersigned, at the Kamo Colliery Office, South British Building, Queen street, Auckland, on Fridays, Saturdays, and Mondays (ONLY), between the hours of 10 a.m. and 3 p.m., or by letter. Mr. Alderton will go to Kaipara, accompanying intending purchasers over the estate.

G. E. ALDERTON.

Agent for Captain W. H. Colbeck.

Auckland, January 28, 1880.

PROOF.

Writing about the quality of this land, Mr. CHAS. E. NELSON, Government Land Purchase Agent, says :—"The soil of these blocks is mostly clay and marl, overlying limestone strata, this fact being a sufficient guarantee of fertility, with at any necessity of allusion to the extraordinary luxuriance of the vegetation generally."

Alderton must have been proud of his employer's performance in parliament. Colbeck was up and down in his seat at every session calling for government expenditure in and around the Kaipara. It was a repeated reminder to the Hall ministry that it was in office because he had changed sides (with three other Northern members) to bring his own government down.

'They want to put it before the country that I am a 'rat',' he told parliament in October 1879, shortly after his election. 'I am only proud to be such a 'rat'.' In November he again defended his actions. He had been charged, he said, with having sold himself for what was called "pelf". But the works account would show whether or not he and other members "had sold themselves to the government for public works."[4] Colbeck's eye for the main chance was only too clear. Railway construction, harbour navigation lights, reduced liquor licence fees for his river steamers — he was so preoccupied with his own (and Kaipara) concerns that when he voted twice against the Property Tax Bill, once as a pair and again in the chamber, it was no doubt "inadvertent," as he claimed.

Only once in his three-year term did Colbeck appear to address a wider issue when he spoke warmly in favour of extending Maori voting rights: "I have some knowledge of the Natives," he said, "considerable numbers of whom live in my district and I claim these men are as fit for the exercise of the vote as I am." It was an impressive democratic stand, marred only by an admission at the end of his speech that he wanted them as additional voters in the north so that it could win more public works than the south! "If I did not openly state that this is my reason. . .I should not be acting honestly and fairly to this house."[5]

Transport was the key to progress as Colbeck tirelessly emphasised. "If you wanted a man to take a sheep," he told parliament, "you paid a shilling to cover expenses." And then again the same week on 40-acre settlers: "As there is no accessible market for anything in Kaipara. . .they must only live on what they can grow, clothing themselves in sheepskins, as certainly no man living at Kaipara could expect to have enough money to pay for a pair of breeches." Not willing to suffer government or private enterprise delays in providing transport, Colbeck established his own Kaipara Steam Navigation Company. Seeking local support, he told a Paparoa meeting early in 1878 that the district should do its own trading "and pocket the profits which now went elsewhere." Of the initial capital of 3000 £1 shares he would contribute a third. Reporting that a bi-weekly service was planned, a *Weekly News* reporter was sceptical:

> To open bright prospects of a successful career before this Company it is only required that we double our population, or start a coal mine, or spirit Captain Casey and his line of boats off the track.

Captain Casey's letter in reply shared the scepticism:

> I have now hanging up in my office a list of 32 bankrupt steam navigation companies. . ...When the company is formed, I hope they will build good boats as, in that case, when the concern gets on its last legs, an offer may be obtained from your most obedient servant, J. Casey.[6]

Within three months an offer was made — not *from*, but *to* Casey, and one he could not refuse. Colbeck bought out his entire fleet of six ships for the enormous sum of £15,000 cash.[7]

The Batley Fish Tinning Factory was set up in the same no-expense- spared manner. The three storey cannery, connected by tramway to the wharf, employed twenty hands and was kept supplied by a dozen fishermen. Leased in 1884 to the partnership of Ewing and Puitarcken (who had run a small cannery alongside the mission station opposite for several years), it processed 80,000 fish, all mullet, the following year. They were packed in hand-soldered 1lb and 2lb tins under the Neptune brand. Some were exported to England.[8]

Neptune fish cannery at Batley.

In 1886 output halved. For over ten years cannery and other fishermen had failed to observe a voluntary closed season during the breeding months and settlers, acting "in a reckless and destructive fashion by netting the mouths of creeks and, for the sake of securing a couple of dozen fish, suffer to be destroyed hundreds of young fish and thousands of spawn."

Some pears and plums were canned to take up the slack — there were plenty available: American fruit was being landed at Auckland cheaper than local orchardists could freight from the Kaipara. Up the Northern Wairoa they were feeding grapes to pigs.

The flour mill fared no better. It too was built on a generous scale with up-to-date machinery and leased to a skilled operator. An English flourmiller, John Linton, who had worked at Lamb's Riverhead mill after a period on the Coromandel goldfield, took over in 1880 and began grinding South Island wheat brought up as ballast on timber ships. This was supplemented by small quantities of local wheat collected by sailing boat from Pakeha and Maori growers. Other mills closer to markets enjoyed the same low inward freight costs and so could undercut Batley flour prices. After two years, full-time production ceased. The Lintons also managed Colbeck's store and hotel and when these were transferred to the first hotel-keeper in the area, Joseph Masefield, in 1884, they moved the mill machinery across the Otamatea to Te

Ihu, their 1000-acre farm leased from Colbeck. Five years later, after intermittent use, the mill finally closed down.[9]

If Batley had become no hub of the universe, the township on Whakapirau creek failed even to get started. A visitor to the area wrote in 1886: "Most of the allotments and sections have been bought by Auckland speculators and absentees, and nothing has been done, somebody apparently waiting for the 'unearned increment.'"[10] That year W.J. Symonds was rafting kauri logs by steam punt to his sawmill at the third town, Karaka (present day Whakapirau), but kauri was in over supply and profits were meagre. The township was not to grow until the timber trade boomed in the Chadwick era. Altogether, Colbeck's "unearned increment" had failed to materialize. As had returns from land sales to migrants or to local targets of Alderton's advertising. "Captain Colbeck's Celebrated Kaipara Limestone Land" was as empty of people as it was when he arrived.

W. H. Colbeck

Colbeck quit the Kaipara after seven years of fruitless hustling. He took court action to recover several thousand pounds loaned on mortgage to Otamatea farmers, he auctioned off his steamship company and he went to Auckland leaving two sons to farm the unsold land. He stood for parliament again, unsuccessfully, in 1887 but in the business world he quickly made his mark as a director of the Bank of New Zealand, the Auckland Milling Company, and other enterprises. He was president of the Chamber of Commerce for a term and president for many years of the Auckland Club. When he died in 1901 flags in the city were flown at half-mast.

Two years after his death the Liberal government acquired the Colbeck estate under the Land for Settlement Act. Some 12,000 acres were subdivided into 51 farms and offered for ballot on 999-year leases. The property was advertised as having "probably sent more fat stock. . .to the markets than any other individual runholder north of Auckland" and was now "suitable for small dairy farms and vineyards."[11] Colbeck's mansion had earlier been split into two houses and moved inland for his sons; now the great woolshed was converted into a house and slowly — leaseholders were wise to be cautious about the future of vineyards — scores of families settled where one family had ruled for almost thirty years.

Hammerhead shark caught in 1885 by the cutter *Elain,*
owned by P. W. Barlow, county engineer.

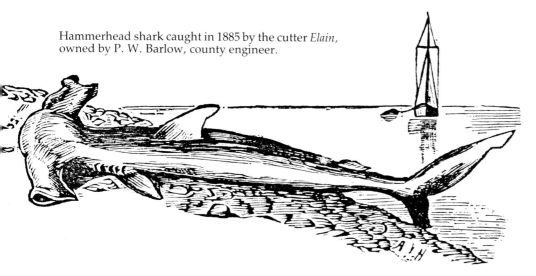

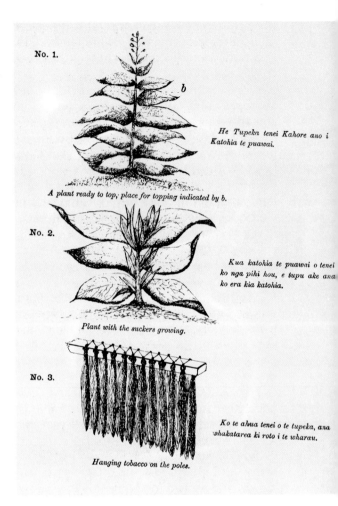

TOBACCO CULTURE

IN

NEW ZEALAND.

INFORMATION AND INSTRUCTION
ON THE
CULTIVATION OF THE TOBACCO PLANT,
COMPILED FROM THE
MOST AUTHENTICATED SOURCES
IN THE TOBACCO-GROWING DISTRICTS IN
NORTH AND SOUTH AMERICA, CUBA, AND THE EUROPEAN COUNTRIES;
ASSISTED BY THE
TWO YEARS' ACTUAL EXPERIENCE
GAINED ON THE
COMPANY'S EXTENSIVE PLANTATION AT PAHI,
ON THE KAIPARA.

BY AUSTIN WALSH.

PRESENTED BY THE
AUCKLAND TOBACCO COMPANY, LIMITED,
FORT STREET, AUCKLAND, N.Z.

Auckland:
PRINTED FOR THE COMPANY BY HERBERT W. FARRINGTON, AT THE
OWL PRINTING WORKS, KARANGAHAPE ROAD.
MDCCCLXXXIV.

No. 1.

b

He Tupeka tenei Kahore ano i Katohia te puawai.

A plant ready to top, place for topping indicated by b.

No. 2.

Kua katohia te puawai o tenei ko nga pihi hou, e tupu ake ana ko era kia katohia.

Plant with the suckers growing.

No. 3.

Ko te ahua tenei o te tupeka, ana whakatarea ki roto i te wharau.

Hanging tobacco on the poles.

A "Pahi Plantation" booklet, 1884, and a page from Grey's Maori pamphlet, 1867.

Another promoter, Austin Walsh, another industry, tobacco, had turned the spotlight on the Kaipara independent of Colbeck's endeavours. Commercial tobacco growing in New Zealand began at Motueka in 1888 according to accepted history, but a tobacco plantation was first planted at Pahi six years before that date.

The company responsible, the Auckland Tobacco Company Ltd, published a substantial booklet in 1884, *Tobacco Culture in New Zealand*, giving instructions on how to cultivate the crop. Prepared by Austin Walsh, the manager, it drew on overseas sources "Assisted by the Two Years' Actual Experience Gained on the Company's Extensive Plantation at Pahi on the Kaipara."

How "extensive" may not have borne examination — Pahi was safely remote from the sceptical — but Austin Walsh's directors included men of substance such as R.C. Barstow, the resident magistrate at Russell, and D.G. Pierce, manager of New Zealand Insurance. Local interests were represented by W.H. Metcalfe of Clairmont, near Matakohe, and George Haines, proprietor of the Pahi general store. Early in 1884 manufacturing premises were being built at Pahi and it was reported that purchases from East Coast growers, mixed with Pahi leaf, would provide sufficient cured tobacco to make a half-million cigars. Good quality cedar boxes had been made ready.[12]

But the company failed. Not because the New Zealand press at that time ran a *British Medical Journal* report that experiments in man and animals had found tobacco to be a "powerful poison," causing cancer of the tongue, lips and other parts of the body.[13] That warning is unlikely to have had any more effect than all those that have followed. Nor was it because the crop did not grow on the Kaipara. Tobacco had been successfully cultivated for home use by local Maoris for years — Sir George Grey had issued an early pamphlet in their language giving instructions. (Like German copra merchants who conducted "smoking schools" in New Guinea, Grey no doubt calculated that addiction would bring dependence on the cash economy.)[14] Whatever the local difficulties — Metcalfe migrated to Australia and Haines accidently shot himself — the tobacco business failed because the mid-eighties was no time to launch any business. The oncoming depression that wracked New Zealand saw to it that of 122 companies formed in Auckland in 1881-85 only five were still operating by 1904.

The Haines store, Pahi, and government "barracks", temporary quarters for the first settlers.

Kaipara ostriches at Whitford Park. The watch was snatched from a reporter.

For Victor Nissen, a Dane rich enough to ignore the economic climate, the Kaipara could yet be made to yield up wealth — dazzling wealth. In 1886 he bought the recently vacated Gittos mission station on the Otamatea, renamed it Aramando Estate, and set about importing ostriches. The arithmetic, according to the *New Zealand Farmer*, was "fabulous." Each female bird averaged thirty eggs a year, therefore a flock of ten females would increase by 300 a year, and at the end of eight years would yield £20,000 of feathers and £200,000 of breeding stock. The wonder of it was that "the capital represented by the flock of birds cannot be lost, nor can the breeder be ruined even if an epidemic should kill all the birds. . .for the reason that a dead ostrich is worth quite as much as a live one."[15]

Sir George Grey was every bit as enthusiastic. Trying to persuade parliament to subsidize Nissen's venture he made a confident prediction:

> There is no fear of the beautiful plumage of the ostrich ever going out of fashion, as the fact of its forming part of the court dress, added to the vested interest not only of the growers but of the wealthy manufacturers and feather dealers is sufficient to put the matter beyond a doubt; and we shall not be surprised to see ostrich farming the most remunerative pastoral industry in the colony.[16]

With that sort of encouragement behind him, Victor Nissen travelled to South Africa to buy breeding stock. The New Zealand government failed to respond to Grey's proposal, however, but not so the South African. It imposed a punitive export duty of £100 per bird to deter newcomers to the industry. (This was the cost of building a standard four-room cottage in New Zealand.)

Nissen was undeterred. Before leaving for South Africa he had written to Grey, "I purpose, not merely as an amateur, to introduce one or two pair of birds, but intend in a. . .substantial manner to enter upon the industry from the outset by importing some 50 to 60 ostriches. . ." This he did. He bought 57 birds and chartered the sailing ship *Johanna Brodersen*, flying the Danish flag, to ship them to New Zealand.

The vessel was fitted out for the voyage with padded stalls, one to each bird, in two rows the length of the ship. A passage six feet (2m) wide ran in front of the stalls and there was drainage at the rear. With stimulant powders in the diet and deodorisers for the drains, Nissen had thought of everything. The live cargo sailed from Durban on 26 November 1886 and the birds were fed eight meals a day, four greens, four grain, with apparently only one dissatisfied passenger, a massively built male bird, "the Drum Major," who from early dawn filled the ship with a "drumming or roaring, deep, prolonged, hollow, and very loud like a lion." The barque ran into storms and one bird jumped five feet out of its stall and another broke loose and raced full speed from one end of the ship to the other, but when the *Johanna Brodersen* reached Kaipara Heads and was towed by steam tugboat to the Otamatea, only eight birds had been lost.[17]

The whole country was watching Nissen's venture. "New Zealand began with the moa; it is to end with the ostrich," a *Lyttelton Times* editorial said. "We give the palm of daring to Mr Nissen. . .to attend a shipload of seasick ostriches." As a later chapter shows, sick New Zealand troops travelling the same route home after the Boer War would have envied the birds.

Importing ostriches to the Kaipara had cost Nissen a fortune. The purchase price of the birds, plus duty, and the cost of transport by South African rail and by chartered ship amounted to £12,000 — equivalent to well over a million dollars today. Farm costs, not least high wire-netting fences, had to be added.

The arithmetic was still promising according to a reporter who visited Nissen's estate in February. An ostrich consumed no more food than a sheep but the sheep gave an annual return of 5/- to 6/- for wool while the ostrich produced feathers valued at £8 to £15. Even a sheep slaughtered for meat returned only 15/- to £1.[18]

The birds were expected to begin laying within a fortnight and incubator-reared young stock were to be exported to San Francisco and Japan. The enterprise, shortly to be honoured by a visit from Sir George Grey, looked fair

The Kaipara was heavily populated by the moa as evidenced by large quantities of gizzard stones. This pile was found on Pahi Peninsula in association with charcoal.

to keep Nissen's promise "to lay at the door of every farmer. . .new sources of wealth and prosperity."

That summer and autumn drought struck the Kaipara. In March it was reported that at Maungaturoto water supplies were failing, crickets were swarming and cattle were in a state of semi-starvation. "What to do nobody appears to know." The first light showers were recorded at Paparoa on 30 April but "the unusually severe drought" continued. In May, Matakohe reported that sheep and cattle had died, that most crops were a failure, gales had brought little rain, it was a terrible season unparalleled in the memory of the oldest settlers." A special correspondent of the *Weekly News* found the ground between the Otamatea and Pahi was cracked open and "gaping with the drought," the creeks were dried up, one settler had lost a hundred sheep. Calling at the ostrich farm he found eggs on sale at a guinea each, "epicures desiring a novelty in omelettes please take notice." There was no comment about the condition of the birds, but ominously, mentioned in passing, was the observation that they were being fed chopped raupo.

Raupo was scarcely the most nutritious of fodders: the farm was in a bad way. Perhaps Nissen did not have a second million on call. He cut his losses that first winter and sold the flock to Auckland merchants L.D. Nathan. Several had died since landing in New Zealand and some sick birds had to be carried on board ship for the journey through the Heads, into the Manukau, and up a tidal inlet to Nathan's Whitford Park farm. A visitor to the farm in mid-June found 43 ostriches installed, three of them "in hospital." The birds were of impressive size, 7 feet 6 inches (2.3m) to the bill with their heads up, but their condition was poor. "The plumage is largely destroyed by the knocking about since leaving Africa and by all accounts their Kaipara home was of the 'Do-the-boys-hall' kind."[19]

Nissen's efforts were not given recognition. And by 1900 when the flock had increased to 500 birds (and a half dozen women were employed dressing feathers for export and making fans) Nathans were claiming the credit for having imported the ostriches — a claim repeated in Lawrence D. Nathan's recent history of the company.[20] The name of Victor Nissen, the man with a great idea gone wrong, deserves a better fate.

Land-jobbing, a tobacco plantation, an ostrich estate — what about the workers? They too had dreams of founding industries, obstinate will in place of bulging wallet, but for all the virtue of hard toil they too failed. One was Alfred Oldham, a Nottinghamshire weaver, who in 1875 purchased William Chadwick's 40-acre grant below Bartons landing at the head of the Pahi River. Oldham had been in the country for sixteen years, one place of employment a flax mill at Kaihu, north of Dargaville. He set up a rough wooden handloom to weave floor coverings from local flax. The raw materials were plentiful and free but coconut fibre could be landed from overseas cheaper than his matting could be freighted from Pahi to Auckland. Efforts to market flax rope and twine were no more successful. He was forced to move closer to the city.[21]

While Oldham was weaving flax, James Wright, a Staffordshire pottery tradesman, was working in clay on the banks of Paparoa Creek, a tidal inlet on the other side of Pahi peninsula. An Albertlander, Wright had operated a kiln in west Auckland for ten years before taking up his land grant. With two sons he produced work of a quality to make him a founding father of New Zealand commercial pottery — a fact that has received recognition only in recent years.[22]

One who appreciated his work at the time was the Rev Allan W. Webb of Auckland who visited the pottery in 1878:

> Hitherto I had seen nothing in the Australasian colonies surpassing in elegance a ginger-beer bottle, a bread pan, or a drain pipe; and, of course expected that the potter's art in such a remote region would have achieved little else. The exterior of the pottery gave but small promise of the wonders which greeted me when I found myself in its interior. A long and low shed, built of roughest material, with a furnace at one end, gave no indication of its being the scene of such labours as would, in the midst of other surroundings, make its occupant famous.

Webb inspected pots at different stages of manufacture. "I was at once astonished at what I saw and could not help looking again and again at the care-worn artist-potter who stood at my side." (An asthmatic, Wright would have had reason to look worn in a dusty shed.) Webb went on to give this tribute:

> Amongst teapots, and jugs, and flower-pots, the articles which most attracted my attention were a row of jugs of terra-cotta ware. . .Here were some jugs with the native flowers of New Zealand curving around them, others with ecclesiastical embossments about them, and each executed with consummate correctness and art — all the man's own workmanship. I felt at once proud and ashamed of New Zealand — proud of its possessing materials and men of such worth, and ashamed that so little encouragement should be afforded such deserving talent.[23]

To promote the sale of jugs, Wright offered to reproduce bas-relief monograms, crests or mottoes of his customers' choice. On the Kaipara few had the means to order such luxuries. Luther Hames, the son of an Albertlander family, who left the district to become a school teacher, has shown the bleak reality in his reminiscences:

> Mr Wright, father of Edward our organist, was a competent potter but the odds were against him. He set up his little works where Mr [Dr?] Dukes lives now and made yellow glazed pipkins and dishes, of which specimens could be seen for years in every house and

A James Wright fruit bowl with damaged lip found at Ruatuna.

39

"Whakapirau River", a painting by Sir William Fox. Colbeck's paper village was on the left.

> dairy for miles around. He got me to write up his venture in the *Weekly* as he wanted a contract to make telegraph insulators, and publicity would help him. I forget if he got the contract. But his venture died a very natural death. Coal, the best clay, and a market, three essentials, were all lacking.[24]

By early 1880, when a royal commission sat to promote New Zealand industry, the county chairman, William Whitaker Ariell gave written evidence that the pottery, like Oldham's rope and matting factory, was "closed from bad roads and heavy freights." And, he said, the local brickyard, its bricks "the best in the Auckland Province," would be obliged to close for the same reasons.

A local reporter used strong language in blaming the government for the 40-acre settlers' isolation:

> The want of progress has been due neither to the inherent natural resources of the land nor the innate energy of the settlers, but to that wretched abortion of a political system which placed a body of strangers on land in the heart of a country without first providing a means of entrance and exit. . .It was one of the most nefarious immigration swindles that ever was perpetrated by a colonial government. They might as well have deluded unsuspecting immigrants to the province by promising them a grant of land in the moon as far as their lifetime was concerned.[25]

A futuristic poem by a local bard, probably J.J. Clark, was passed around in handwritten copies at this time. Its description of disaster came uncomfortably close to the truth for the Kaipara. The poem's inspiration was a much-discussed article in the English *Blackwood's Magazine* which reported the downfall of the

40

British Empire after defeat in an imaginary battle of "Dorking." Time, it could be said, has brought the poem even closer to the truth for Britain.

> Now Pahi hall a ruin lies, and though 'tis a disgrace,
> We've never had the means to build another in its place.
> For 'tis not now as once it was ere Dorking's fatal field
> Announced to all the nations that Great Britain's fate was sealed.
>
> For ere that time when we had spent all the means at our command
> We asked and she supplied our wants with free maternal hand.
> But now beneath a load of debt, this hapless country groans,
> Nor can we pay our interest off by raising other loans.
>
> For from the place she once maintained, Old England has been thrust,
> Her greatness, power and lofty pride lie prostrate in the dust.
> And conquered is that noble land, once mistress of the seas,
> Whose flag had braved a thousand years, the battle and the breeze.
>
> Still, though in shattered fragments lie her palaces and halls,
> No painter has as yet portrayed the ruins of St Pauls.
> But if I should be spared, my dears, that mournfull day to see,
> I'd stake my life the artist is a native of Pahi.[26]

J.J. Clark, married to an Albertlander's daughter, did not stay around to check his fanciful predictions; he joined the exodus of the eighties and moved inland to Omaru, (now Ararua). A pity, a Pahi River Anthology on the facts of his neighbours' lives could have been as engagingly off-beat as his fiction.

Another dream. Thomas Downes drilling for oil on Paparoa Creek.

The crowd, animated and concentrated, two views of the 1915 regatta by Percy Stevens. Note his action shot of the greasy boom.

Men, Horse & Dog Swimming Races
  Decided on the motion of Mr Hemphill seconded by Mr Colbeck, That Mr G Jackman start the above Races, and that Mr R C Smith be asked to Judge the Events. carid

From the 1913 minute book.

3. The great Pahi Regatta
& other diversions

Then everyone, masters, mistresses, children and servants, turn out . . .everyone seems light-hearted and happy on a Pahi sports day.
— P.W. Barlow, *Kaipara*, 1888

I remember intoxicating evenings in my childhood when from the peace of the Kaipara river I heard the Otamatea Maori band and the glorious singing in the villages on the little river bays. Are there any native bands now? And if so why were they not at the celebration?

Jane Mander on Waitangi Day, 1934

"The one day of the year at Pahi and then to sleep again." Percy Stevens, photographer, pencilled this comment on the back of a 1913 regatta scene of a densely crowded domain with a packed flag-ship at the wharf. "Altogether it [Whakapirau] was a very isolated area and only seemed to come alive on Annual Regatta Day," a school teacher, Miss B.L. Pitney, wrote in 1974 when looking

A turn-of-century race, *Viking*, built 1897, (centre) behind *Olive* (brown sails). Another yacht is obscured by ss *Gosford* at Pahi wharf.

back almost half a century to the years 1925-28 when she was in sole charge of the combined Pahi-Whakapirau school. And what was true on the land applied equally to the waterways of the Kaipara. Except for the years when the mill was ripping through kauri and tall masts from across the world were always nudging around bends in the river, the waters of the north-east Kaipara ebbed and flowed largely undisturbed. But on regatta day, and the day before and the day after, the tranquillity seemed shattered forever. Particularly before the event when craft of

Jane Mander left the Kaipara at 18; this photo taken a few years later.

The Pooks' *Thistle,* a regatta winner when sailed by the Curels. She was wrecked on Manukau bar in 1953.

all kinds purposefully converged on Pahi with an expectancy that electrified the harbour air.

Jane Mander has described the many arms that make the harbour: "There was something fascinating about seeing a little trickle of water grow until it could carry an ocean-going ship. She [the heroine of *The Strange Attraction*] loved the places that rivers came from, the mangrove swamps they cut across, the lagoons they sneaked out of, the gullies they watered."

These were the inlets that on regatta day disgorged whaleboats, skiffs and punts, sailboats and yachts, pleasure launches and truant members of the fishing fleet. They moved into the mainstream and formed mini-processions that travelled in the wake of steamers from Helensville and Dargaville, one a flag-ship smothered in bunting and ringing to the sound of a brass band. There were contests to be fought on land: not just athletics but chain stepping, nail driving, wood chopping, horse jumping, potato peeling and cutting the ham. From guessing a sheep's weight to catching the greasy pig, something for everyone. In contests at sea, yachts and launches churned the water and oarsmen bent their backs over gruelling one and two mile courses. Suspended over water was the long greasy boom, competitors braved the lung-testing corfu dive and swimming races were run for men, horses and dogs. The horses swam the half-mile from Whakapirau to Pahi, riders mounted bare-back on entering and leaving the water but hanging to the tail during the race, leaning one way or another to steer like a

Under the Moreton Bay fig, 1921; donkey rides, 1918; tug-of-war (without a rope) 1921.
Percy Stevens photographs.

rudder. It was a great crowd pleaser but hard on the horses, many said cruel, and children cried to see them flogged as they floundered out through the mud. In 1923 the race was caught by an outgoing tide, horses trapped in mud nearly drowned, the SPCA became involved, and the event was discontinued.

Competitions apart, the domain was alive with entertainment — and not only at the hotel where roaring bar and billiard room were packed tight and beer was served straight out of open windows to the beach front. For the crowds on the green or in the shade of the Moreton Bay fig the brass band on the flag-ship came ashore to play and there were sideshows and roundabouts, donkey rides and lolly scrambles, and pedlars with glittering wares. A fortune teller's tent was among the sideshows and a shooting gallery, coconut shy, ball-and-pin game, "Aunt Sally" and "Mr Spon Dulicks."[1] This latter booth, like the others, presumably took more money than it gave, and so it was just as well that tickets to the concert and dance that followed the regatta were sold in advance. In a typical year (1915) 300 tickets were printed for the steamer, 500 for the grounds and 150 for a nights revelry that ended at daylight. As the local bard said:

> Oh 'twas a gallant sight to see, our Pahi youths so stout,
> How soon they triumphed o'er and cut poor Matakohe out.
> Took all the partners for themselves, Outsiders had no show,
> We gave all the other places 'fits', some sixty years ago.
>
> Thus all the night, with keen delight, they danced until the sun
> Announced, with clear and ruddy beams, another day begun.
> Forth then they sallied and embarked upon the limpid tide
> And with light hearts, but wearied limbs, slowly homeward hied.

Just how slowly in the early days is told in the Linnell diary. George Linnell, his son, young George, and four others left their farm on the Otamatea to attend the Pahi Sports as it was then called, in 1886. They had ten miles (16k) to row and three days were taken up attending a one-day event, including a night on the beach waiting for the tide. The diary gives a matter-of-fact record:

Another regatta scene by Percy Stevens. At far right, opposite shore, is Jackman's old store.

Watching the four-oared gig race. A Frank Blackwell photo.

Monday: Borrowed boat from the Maoris and six of us went to the Pahi or rather started for it. We got to Batley about 12oc.
Tuesday: Stayed on the beach at Batley till about 4oc and then started for Pahi. Got there about 6oc in the morning, they were all very much surprised to see us as they thought we would have ridden. The sports were very good. . .George and I went to the McMurdo's early and went to bed, the others went to the entertainment in the evening.
Wednesday: Started for home about 12oc am, the Hargreaves started the same time — stayed at Batley 2 or 3 hours and got home about 8oc pm. Beautiful weather all the time.
Thursday: George took the boat back as far as Lintons for the Maoris, Miss Ryan went down with them for the pull. Saw some peaches on the other side but had nothing to get them in.[2]

At this time, Maori contestants carried off many of the prizes. Hori, Wiremu, Niho and others identified by first name only, regularly won the 100-and 200-yard events, the shot put, pole vault and high jump — and three-legged races. Perhaps Niho was present when the Arapaoa Maori church was opened in 1878 (to the sound of singing items by Pakeha ladies) and the elders "exhorted the youth present. . .to excel in all English Customs."[3] At the next sports, in addition to athletic success, he won the boating race of the day, a two-mile punt race, first prize a handsome £2/10/-.

At the church opening the elders had also exhorted the young to excel "above all in kindness to their friends — the white people." This was not to be at the 1880 sports. Star attraction was a four-oared gig race, first prize £6, and the two Maori entrants refused to start in protest at the handicapping. One of the boats was unaffected but it withdrew in support of the other. And entry fees

Regatta parking, horseless carriages nearest the action.

for the athletics had been raised. Objecting to the charges, Maori competitors boycotted several events. Maori boys, however, came first and second in the junior 100 yards, Niho won the shot put and "George (Maori)" won the 150 yards maiden race and the 100 yards open handicap. And winning the pole vault, "George, who was in sporting costume, vaulted very gracefully and succeeded in reaching 7 feet 11 inches (2.28m)." Despite the partial boycott, Maori prizewinners collected £8/15/- "and yet," it was sourly observed, "as entrance money among the whole number, the large sum of 5/- was all the money subscribed."[4] The problem of Maori youth monopolizing the prizes

Away from the hubbub. A 1905 regatta day study.

was solved in future years (well into the 20th century) by dividing childrens and junior races, both girls and boys, into two events, "Native" and "European."

At the concert that night a popular performer on the mouth-organ was the Austrian "naturalist," Andreas Reischek. He had been staying for several weeks with first Edward and then Thomas Coates, spending his time robbing burial sites and dynamiting for fossils. In his case, the elders' injunction of kindness to white friends was apparently heeded.[5]

By 1886 boating events were overshadowing athletics and that year the Pahi Regatta Club was established. Dr John Mountaine, who had just completed the first year of a subscription-based medical service, was first president. Whakapirau farmer William Upton was secretary. In over ten years of informally run annual sports much groundwork had already been laid — not least in the field of refreshments. Batley Hotel had been closed down in 1876 on representations from William Gittos who complained of "nocturnal visits" from its customers to the pupils of Tanoa School. He also charged that grog had been sold illegally to Maoris "supplied in order to secure cheap land bargains." With Batley dry, the club took on new importance. Committee meetings, attended in later years by 50 or 60 members, were conducted like smoke concerts. At one period Matakohe, Batley, Maungaturoto, Hukatere and Ararua were all sending two delegates each.

A northern publican in 1877 had gained a licence to sell spirits on the day. "A great deal of excitement was caused the Good Templars," one paper reported, but temperance people "were more frightened than hurt." There was more drunkenness at the previous sports when bottles had to be planted in the scrub. By 1882, when

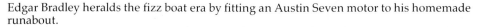

Edgar Bradley heralds the fizz boat era by fitting an Austin Seven motor to his homemade runabout.

Walsh Brothers fly in the first seaplane, 1921, and a Maori boy quickly produces a colourable imitation.

Pahi Hotel was operating on Batley's transferred licence, the laid-back shambles that was to pass for organization in the years ahead was well installed. The ss *Tangihua* arrived from the Northern Wairoa with twenty members of the Aratapu Choral Society on board under the leadership of John Chadwick — a refining presence that did not deter the passengers from making "a rush for the hotel." The committee must have been ahead of them for the first event started over an hour late and of £60 in prizemoney only £40 was distributed as darkness fell before the programme could be completed. The greatest (official) amusement of the day came from the greasy pole contest, won by a Maori.[6]

Pahi Hotel was closed shortly after "on account of being ill-conducted" and the ratepayers voted to keep it shut for the next three years. A year before the time was up, Ebenezer Hadrill, providore of the Northern River Steam Navigation Company, applied for the licence. Accommodation was needed for the passengers on the ss *Minnie Casey*, he said. Pahi was a healthy, pleasant summer resort and good sea bathing was possible close to the hotel. As proof of the tight ship he would keep "he intended to establish bathing machines as at Cheltenham Beach." Hadrill was granted a licence with ten o'clock closing. There is no record of local limbs being shielded from public view in bathing machines but not long after the *Minnie Casey* was caught selling whiskey at Topuni mill, a piece of regular sly-grogging brought to notice when one customer drowned from a punt. Hadrill's company was fined £10, the maximum under the Licencing Act.

Putting down boyhood memories in 1963-4, Brian W.H. Smith, school teacher grandson of Richard and Catherine Smith, pioneer Matakohe sawmillers, told how committee and competitors floated through regatta day, even in the 20th century:

> For those with salt blood in their veins, the annual Otamatea Regatta held at Pahi was certainly the highlight of the year. . .There was always plenty of excitement at these functions: with a wide variety of competitions both on water and on land. The launch races provided no speed thrills, but the lumbering craft, chiefly working launches, plugged sedately around the course, the officials themselves generally being in doubt as to the actual winner. However, some befuddled handicapper would finally work out the place-getters with occasionally the last boat to cross the line being the winner.
>
> The hotel was, of course, the Mecca of many thirsty souls and the local police officers often had to recourse to stern measures to keep the peace. Fights were common, and much entertainment was provided by the soaks endeavouring to return to their launches moored offshore. "Crabs" were caught by bleary oarsmen who often finished up in the water with the thick layer of tenacious salt mud adding to their difficulties.
>
> A useful grandstand was provided by the flagship, usually the *Wairua* or the *Ruawai* which made special trips from Dargaville for the occasion. Failing these, the old *Tuirangi*, arrayed in all the bunting she possessed, filled the bill. With all the spectators thronging to the seaward side to view the finish of aquatic events, it was only the mooring ropes that prevented the vessel from heeling over.[7]

Placed in its Kaipara perspective, regatta day was almost a decorous affair. It was an age of drinking to oblivion as shown by this *Weekly Herald* report of how hotels were being conducted around the harbour:

> It is customary for the barkeeper, when the men get to the 'fresh' stage, to run up lattice work specially made for the purpose, as guards to the windows and bar furniture; but when 'the heroes of a hundred drunks' are helplessly prone on the floor, under the combined influence of 'tanglefeet' and 'rot-gut', a couple of stretcher men speedily whip away the 'dead drunk' off to an outbuilding in the rear . . . known as 'the dead house', there to sleep off the effects of the debauch. On one Sunday, 18 bushmen and gumdiggers were lying 'heads and tails' in the deadhouse, having been run in early in the day, while in an adjoining room a parson was holding forth on 'the Fall of Man'. . .[8]

Coping well — at this early stage. Guy Jackman, regatta club president for 40 years (right) and officials Dave McCarroll and Bunnie Tilby.

The tide rules. *Tui* caught on the Otamatea, and Pahi Hotel marooned in 1938 by a king tide and strong south-westerlies.

Another report spoke of how drunken scenes in the streets around the Native Land Court in Helensville "did not bear description" while Pakeha gumdiggers were also "lying hopelessly stupefied. . .in the fern and the ditches on the banks of the Awaroa." The death of a boatload of drunken mourners returning from a funeral on the Northern Wairoa prompted a newspaper calculation that drownings on the Kaipara, almost all due to drink, had averaged one a month for several years. A rival newspaper called this hurtful to relatives and claimed that horseplay and poor boatmanship were responsible. The Port Albert writer of a letter-to-the-editor, as anonymous as he or she was smug, made this scornful reply:

> How is it that the Albertland settlers are never scandalized with the occurrence of such tragedies. . .? Have they no dangers to encounter in traversing in their boats the Oruawharo, the Otamatea and the Arapaoa? Is it that the Albertlanders refrain from 'chaffing', 'keep their tempers' and 'sit still' when boating?[9]

The answer, of course, was that "their immunity from such calamities" was because they had "banished intoxicating liquors."

Intoxication comes in different forms, it later emerged. Some so-proper Albertlanders sought oblivion in ways that "scandalized" the whole country. Planned as an unsectarian Christian community founded on co-operative principles, Port Albert had been divided by what one of the architects of toleration, Rev Dr Samuel Edgar, called the "straitest sect." Extreme religious fervour led to religious hysteria and a five day "holiness camp meeting" in 1884 received nationwide publicity. Over 200 people took part, including visitors from Auckland attending a temperance rally, and a visiting American evangelist touched off such frenzy among them that even the sober *Herald* reported

Unwelcome publicity for the Albertlanders. An extract from this 1884 pamphlet below.

A MEMORABLE SUNDAY.

On Sunday, November 30th, the excitement reached a climax. The scene at the Camp on that day beggars description.

Between two and three o'clock in the afternoon the greatest excitement prevailed, men were howling and yelling like maniacs, women were running about and screaming and as mad as March hares, while young girls employed themselves in tearing up their clothes seemingly utterly regardless of decency. Indeed the women, carried away by the excitement, appeared to be lost to all sense of shame, and openly indulged in words and actions which they would, at any other time, have been horrified at the thought of.

Four times one woman rushed out of the tent, screaming, "Come to Jesus! come to Jesus!" and four times she had to be carried back by main force. The husband, when appealed to, declined to interfere, attributing his wife's condition "to the Holy Spirit, nothing more."

Another unfortunate woman was in violent hysterics, and in fact, for the time, a raving maniac. About five o'clock she darted out of her sleeping tent and seized hold of a Mr. Hamilton, who, after struggling with her, carried her into the tent, where (the gentleman afterwards said) he had half-a-dozen mad people dancing round him, praying, singing, and yelling. When he tried to leave they called upon

God to "root him on his knees to the Spot,"

and screamed, "God strike him there, and do not suffer him to move."

Scandulos Goings On.

On this memorable Sunday night the goings on at the camp were positively scandalous. Lost to all feelings of propriety some of the women openly made proposals which can only be characterised as disgraceful in the extreme. One misguided woman vainly endeavoured to lure a gentleman into her sleeping tent, more than hinting her desires and saying that she would be held blameless if she indulged them!

THE KISS OF PEACE.

About three o'clock on the morning of Monday the sleepers (there were not many!) were aroused by the yells of a woman who appeared to be but scantily clad and who was wandering about in the rain calling out aloud that she had "lost shame for Jesus' sake," and other things I will not particularize. The poor creature then flung herself in the mud, and her friends would not allow her be "touched;" she was at length carried into her tent by a man who insisted on her removal from the mire, and who, pitying the state of the poor soul, would have his own way in the matter in spite of her husband and friends. While the mad woman was lying on the ground in dishabille, Brother Thomas came out (with very little on) and administered "the kiss of peace."

AS SWEET AS HONEY!

One man was boasting about having exchanged the "Holy Kiss" with "Brother Thomas," and appealed to that worthy to verify his statement. The Holy Man yelled back the kiss was as "sweet as honey" and that "if he had a million pounds he would give it for another such a kiss" ! ! !

proceedings in detail and editorialised on behaviour that "made a mockery of all that is sacred." Nothing like it had ever been recorded anywhere else in New Zealand, said the *Herald*. Its local correspondent added: "A few of the quiet and sane inhabitants here would heartily rejoice could the whole proceedings be utterly blotted out of all human recollection."[10]

The issue of a pamphlet, *Naughty Doings at Port Albert*, put paid to that hope. The pamphlet may have been sensation-mongering (see opposite) but in fact events reached such a pitch that the local constable was forced to call for reinforcements. Naming some prominent citizens, he telegraphed his superintendent, "To the best of my belief [they] are complete maniacs and it is impossible for me to attend to them all."[11] It was not a good time for the self-righteous. Only a week before the Maungaturoto parson, Rev Abraham Riding, had been arrested on a ship while trying to escape prosecution for homosexual offences with a minor; his church mysteriously burned down a few months later. It had not been wise to cast the first stone at plain, honest-to-goodness drunks.

Perhaps the middle ground may be safely occupied by this celebration of a social event in 1912.

The spree was at the Pahi pub
To farewell Jim, the gallant sub,
For other reasons, as you'll hear,
Men turned up from far and near.

Te kai, kapai, waipiro plenty.
Advice to you, who bottle empty
When full of ink, to walk unable,
Don't hesitate but try the stable.

The chairman Coates, brand new MP,
Father Jackman on the spree,
Martin, old boy, full of pepper,
Ancient Stoney should know better.

Hemphill, Baff and Captain Sellars
And scores of other jolly fellows,
Sterling, he who makes the butter,
"Whusky's guid", was heard to mutter.

Then to dance with ladies fair,
Sisters, cousins, aunts, were there.
Somehow nearly all connected,
If I'm wrong I stand corrected.

To dance and sing and make a noise
Husbands, lovers, men and boys,
More than one old grey stager
All to honour the Sergeant-Major.

Strangers there from Parts Remote,
"Te Hana" wouldn't sing a note.
The "Aged One" he danced his best
With intervals for drink and rest.

Jim left the next morning sore at heart,
'Twas ever thus when friends do part.
Behind were left some heads as sore
And that is what the spree was for.

Edith and Heathcote Jackman and their children, George, Ernest, Mary, Guy and Alice (sitting). Eric was born later.

4. *He made the vine flourish*

Heathcote Jackman was a farmer more than a fortune-hunter, and that set him apart from the flock of predators, public school boys in the main, who descended on the north-east Kaipara in the sixties and seventies. Most came as younger sons of the gentry who had missed out on the first line of inherited wealth and who did not fancy (or were ineligible for) the standard bolt-holes of their kind, army, navy, church and colonial service. Their aim was to amass large sums of money as quickly as possible and return to England to upstage their older brothers. It could be successful on vast South Island grazing runs or on sweeping tracts of confiscated Maori land in the North Island — but not on the sleepy banks of the Otamatea and Te Pahi rivers.

One by one, sooner or later, the sons of empire moved to pastures more promising. One of the earliest, Lewis Rye, who came on the *Blue Jacket* in 1860 moved on — after planting gorse — to British Columbia, as did his Otamatea neighbour, Timothy Hull. C.J. Metcalfe returned to England after ten years (his wife could not accustom herself to the lack of servants, it was said), Harry Eastman became a Canterbury sheep farmer, William Colbeck a director of Auckland companies, Thomas Coates a gentleman-farmer stud-breeder on the edge of Auckland. And, after working in partnership with W.H. Jackman for a few years, Robert Ernest Jackman left his brother to it.

For many of them the Kaipara episode was something of a lark, the big break away from home. The experiences of a half-dozen such young men, "entitled" in their own words, "to the designation gentleman," has been set down in the two-volume *Brighter Britain! or Settler and Maori in Northern New Zealand.* Written by William Delisle Hay, this rare book is centred on the Pahi River where its heroes, given pseudonyms,[1] lived in smoke-filled shanties, slept on potato sacks stuffed with fern and "mounga" and sat on kegs and boxes. They ate with sheath knives, wooden skewers and fingers. There was only one fork between them "and that only a prong and a half remaining." The food was better this way than served up on fine china or silver, ". . .meat is meat still, although it may be eaten direct out of a frying-pan or stew-pot."

> Our custom is to wear our clothes just as long as they will hold together. . .there is no time for mending in the bush, so we are often rather ragged. Washing is a nuisance. . ..Frequent washing spoils clothes and causes them to rot sooner. Besides it is unnecessary where there are no woman about. . ..Razors, of course, were discarded long ago. . .

Smelly, ragged, unshaven and rejoicing in squalor, what better way for poor-little-rich-boys to say "bum" to mummy. Their mentor in all things was Old Colonial, the name given to W.H. Jackman, "a burly, bearded man" who had been at the same school as the author — in the sixth form when Hay was in the first. "It was owing to his letters home that we had determined on emigration."

Jackman came to New Zealand on the *Chile* in 1866 when he was twenty. He had money to spend, as much as £2000 (his home on the edge of the New Forest was a mansion, in American hands today, and his mother, a James of St Andrews, Scotland, was wealthy in her own right), but he was practical, energetic and resourceful. On his father's side he came from farming stock and he topped off his education at an agricultural school on Jersey Island before working on a farm for two years.[2]

"The acute and wise diplomatist" in Hay's phrase, he had a knack of getting along with the local Maori people. He picked up enough of the language to converse easily, he learned something of the customs and legends and, being a single man, could circulate rather amiably among daughters of the tribe. Arama Karaka, the Ngati Whatua chief, talked to him "as one chief among men may talk to another," says Hay. He often propounded to Jackman his "pet theory. . ..to save the Maori from dying out."

> Lo! the Pakeha men are very many. It is good that they should see our maidens, and it is good that they should marry them. Then there will be children that shall live, and a new race of Maori blood. So there shall be some to say that in time to come, 'This is the land of our mothers. This was the land of the Maori before the Pakeha came out of the sea.'

Karaka's offer of land as a dowry failed to tempt the young gentlemen according to Hay. "We have tried to urge the Little 'Un [Harry Eastman] or the Saint [Ernest Jackman] or even O'Gaygun [Nicholas Martin] into some such match; but they are shy, I suppose, and do not seem to fancy taking 'a savage woman to rear their dusky race.' Yet it would be unfair to call the brunette beauties of Tanoa savages." Old Colonial's response is not recorded. Jackman paid the full price (£2 an acre) for the 1000-acre Akahiwi block, which included the great Marahemu pa site and fronted on the water immediately up-river from present day Whakapirau. He also acquired, less expensively it is said, 500 acres at Naumai in part furtherance of the "fusion between the races" policy of the Ngati Whatua.

Jackman's good standing with the Maori was duplicated with the Pakeha. Hay again: "His experience and acumen have made him a general referee among the Kaipara settlers; and in all important matters, he is usually the interpreter and spokesman between them and the natives." Hay was an acurate observer. In 1883, a year after his book was published, Jackman was elected to represent Whakapirau riding on Rodney County Council. And in 1887, when Otamatea county was formed, he was re-elected, missing the dead-heated chairmanship only after the two names had been placed in "the deepest bell-topper to be found

The county chairman, W. Heathcote Jackman, framed by the council door, and councillors.

among the councillors' hats." The events surrounding that dramatic moment were related by the *Auckland Weekly News:*

> A much respected and well known resident of Paparoa volunteered to find an eligible person to draw, and hurriedly left the hall for that purpose. Descrying a workman halfway up a ladder he immediately hailed and requested him to come and draw lots for the chairman of the Otamatea Council.
> The gentleman on the ladder (probably on account of the incessant hammering) evidently only imperfectly heard, for he called out to his mate on the roof, "My eye, Bill! here's a go. They wants me to be Chairman of the Otamatea Council!" The individual in the elevated regions, after due reflection, replied, "You take my advice, Jack, and have nothing to do with 'em." This advice Jack concluded to follow, and refused to leave the ladder for the chair. Eventually the services of a small boy were secured, and Mr Isbister returned as chairman.[3]

Jackman, now a justice of the peace, was married with a young family. His wife Edith was a striking woman, her looks owing something to the Spanish blood in her family, the Hargreaves of the 8,500-acre Puketotara block down-harbour at Oneriri. Brother Ernest had departed but the household included another younger brother, Frank, a confirmed bachelor, sent out from England "to get away from it" — Victorian double-speak for the exile of alcoholic sons. It meant "get into it — away from us." Francis James Jackman had a fine tenor voice — he had sung with the famed Lily Langtry — but he was a classic remittance man. He often failed to return after his monthly visit to Auckland for a bank draft. His brother could always find him — in a police cell at the end of a drinking binge. An amiable man, Frank Jackman's exploits in crossing the harbour to Pahi Hotel — whether by casting adrift a timber barge at the mill and floating with the tide, or straddling a log and paddling — have gone into local legend.

W.H. Jackman tried to duplicate English farming methods, but like his neighbours, found English crops a failure. Livestock farming brought thin profits because of distance from markets. And so he diversified into gum buying, acquired blocks of land as far afield as the Otamatea and sold them off, and opened a store on the beach in front of Heathcote, his double-storey house. He sailed a scow around the harbour delivering stores and collecting gum for direct export to England. The business flourished and several trips were made to the "Old Country." The little store on the beachfront became hopelessly inadequate. The only place to expand was in the empty bay a few hundred yards along the shoreline — present-day Whakapirau. Marked on the first map in 1858 Wahi Tapu, sacred place, the bay remained forbidden to all-comers. Bones from the great Ngapuhi slaughter of 1825 were still wedged in trees and littered the ground. Jackman had explained the situation in the seventies to his young gentlemen friends:

> The chiefs won't sell an inch of this piece to anyone; and not a Maori dares go near it. Lots of people have tried to buy it, and have even offered as much as five pounds an acre for its magnificent soil; but the Maoris are not to be tempted, and, what's more, say they'll have utu from any Pakeha that goes onto it.

Jackman accepted its unavailability with good grace:

> We ought to keep alive the memories that make the place romantic. . .. No need to make a commonplace farm out of that picturesque old battle-ground. May it long remain just as it is now — a lovely natural monument to ancient Maori valour, a quiet undisturbed resting place for the warrior dead, the patriot chivalry of the Ngati Whatua.[4]

But the situation had changed. Captain Colbeck in his headlong drive to organize a "special settlement" had scooped up the land by building a mausoleum for the bones. It was a handsome, chapel-like building constructed of stone with buttressed walls. The internal walls were lined of shelves, the skulls were prised out of tree forks, the bones were gathered up and the ancestors of the Ngati Whatua were stacked inside. Whether Gittos performed the ceremonies is not known. It is hard to believe that the man who presided at every religious event missed this profound occasion.

Heathcote and the first beachfront store.

The mausoleum that lifted tapu from the land. (Blackwell photo)

The mausoleum stood among cabbage trees on high ground overlooking the harbour. In photographs its gothic lines and its thick-walled sombre aspect exude an ecclesiastical presence every bit as powerful as that of the Gittos "cathedral" at Tanoa. What need for tapu over the land where the remains rested in such Christian care? Symonds's timber mill at Pahi was moved across to the new site, Jackman built a bigger general store and gum-trading depot there, residential sections were subdivided, a boarding house and livery stables were erected, later to become the home of Jackman's son, Guy. (It still stands, much modified.) The new village was called Karaka, the name of the chief who had always collaborated so well with the Pakeha. The honour was a brief one. It appears on some maps but Karaka was also the old name for Drury, Thames, and other places in both islands and the post office required a change. The name Whakapirau was taken from Whakapirau Creek, down-harbour where Colbeck had planned yet another village.

In 1890, after seven years of local body service, Jackman's place was taken by the Colbeck brothers, sons of the departed entrepreneur. Arthur Colbeck represented Whakapirau riding for two terms, 1890-96, and then Frank Colbeck took over for two, 1896-1902. Jackman was then re-elected. During his 12-year gap in public service he unsuccessfully stood for parliament. The sitting member, Richard Monk, defeated him at the 1896 general election. Out of office, three of his four sons growing old enough to run the farm and business, W. Heathcote

The Adams house, an 1874 watercolour.

Jackman had time and energy to spare. It was poured into the establishment of a model vineyard.

On paddocks behind the house where he had first tried to grow wheat (and had finally settled for oats) he now planted grapes. It was the first stage fulfilment of a Kaipara prophecy. As early as the '70s the author of *Brighter Britain!* had observed how grapes were "very luxuriant" on the Pahi River. "This will be the wine country of the future," he predicted. "Already some people at Mangawhai have made good wine and have started a little trade in it." In fact, Wendolin Albeitz and his wife Ursalina had planted grapes for wine making at Mangawhai in 1860. By 1875 they were growing fifteen different varieties on three acres and were pressing 1500 gallons each vintage. Four other settlers brought the vineyard area to eight acres, the largest concentration in the country at that time, but the fungus disease oidium soon after destroyed all their work.[5]

On the Hokianga the Germans, Heinrich Breidecker and Carl Schrieder, were making wine in commercial quantites in the eighties, as were three Swiss, Rous, Wolff and Heiber, at Helena Bay, north of Whangarei. The vintner's skills, it seemed, were the province of "foreigners." But Englishmen could learn the secrets. Down at Te Hana, the Albertlander Charles Levet and his son William learned from a translation of a French textbook. Jackman bought a small library of translated French works.[6] He was after finer vintages than his neighbours.

English country wines were to be found in every farm kitchen. Fruit wines, perry, cider, mead, the lethal sounding metheglin (a spiced or medicated mead) all competed at the North Kaipara Show. Even that scourge of demon drink, the Gittos household, won prizes for peach wine and sugar beer. (Their mead had merits too. The runholder Hargreaves was once unable to rise from his chair after drinking at their table.)[7] Ernest Adams, a prominent Methodist, always took the grape wine prize. Victorian hypocrisy, in an attitude that has endured, put wine in a different category from its potent sister products. Adams extended operations to a double-storey winery which housed the winepress on the ground floor with its screw reaching into the floor above. The lever was long enough for three people to push it around to crush the grapes below. This was no domestic husbandry, he had become a serious winemaker, so serious that at election time he always left his prohibitionist wife and daughters behind when he rowed across to Pahi to vote.[8]

Much of the district's output was sold — illegally — to gumdiggers, bushmen, millworkers and seamen on the timber ships, but whether cloudy or clear, sweet or extra sweet, the name wine was often a courtesy title. All this changed after the visit in 1895 of the Italian viticulturist Romeo Bragato. His highly favourable report brought a wave of grape planting throughout the country. A North Auckland Vinegrowers' Association was formed to launch the industry around the Kaipara and 30,000 cuttings were distributed to its 50-odd members. At the association's second annual meeting, held at Whakapirau in 1898, initial steps were taken to establish a "co-operative wine factory" to be run along the lines of farmer-owned dairy factories. Jackman was elected president.[9] The following year he was given the rare honour of a full page photograph in the annual report of the Department of Agriculture. He was shown standing among two-year-old vines that had produced "abundant foliage" from cuttings supplied by a government experimental station in Hawkes Bay. Only one cloud hung over a bright horizon — phylloxera. Bragato had discovered that the deadly aphid that had ravaged Europe was present in New Zealand and recommended use of resistant vines. The Department of Agriculture failed to follow his advice. Phylloxera spread. In the summer of 1898-99 two vine inspectors made a house-to-house search of the vineyard areas of Northland. Lightly infected vines were to be treated, those badly diseased were to be destroyed.

Inspector Potter made this report:

> *Otamatea County.* I commenced at Whakapirau, finding a large quantity of vines cultivated: Mr Jackman, 4 1/2 acres of trained vines, about six thousand; Mr McMurdo, next neighbour, 3 acres of vines, about four thousand. These gentlemen are the principal growers in this county. The whole of their vines I found free of disease. They both gave me every assistance in showing me who had vines, and directed me to those who lived in out-of-the-way places. I inspected about twelve thousand in this county. At the request of Messrs Jackman and McMurdo, I went with them and examined those infested places across the river, previously reported by Mr Harnett, all bad with disease.

Inspector Harnett's report confirmed just how bad:

> In January, 1899, I went to Pahi, Otamatea County. In this place I totally eradicated the vines on four properties, one of which contained an area of 1 1/2 acres, which was nothing better than a wilderness and had to be trenched in a face from end to end.[10]

The names of the infected vineyards were not given but presumably some or all were those of "Austrians," reported in 1896 to be "beginning to cultivate the vine on an extensive scale" at Pahi. "Austrians" were Dalmatians and "Pahi" as a postal address then included Hukatere where ex-gumdiggers had settled.

Cellars, vineyard and views of Heathcote, a wash drawing from the *Graphic* by E. B. Vaughan, 1900.

Jackman, meanwhile, went from strength to strength. The *Graphic* featured his vineyard in glowing terms in 1900. An artist's full-page illustration caught not only the feel of cellar and vineyard but surely placed the enterprise in its idyllic Kaipara setting. The accompanying article read:

> Everywhere. . .the settlers are putting in vines, encouraged by the signal success of those who have already done so. For this state of things, and for the increased prosperity which must soon follow, Mr Walter [sic] Heathcote Jackman is practically alone responsible. . . .He has. . .without ceasing preached the gospel of viticulture and practiced what he preached. Discouragements only seemed to whet his enthusiasm, and he persevered and possessed his soul in patience when things went wrong. . .so that he is now the largest and most successful vine-grower up North. . . .Mr Jackman may, therefore, be given some considerable kudos for starting the North on a new and sure road towards a solid and ever-increasing prosperity. Other enthusiastic growers in the district are Mr H. McMurdo and genial Dr Montaigne [sic] of Maungaturoto.[11]

Jackman's influence extended far beyond the north. He read a paper on winemaking to the annual conference of the Fruitgrower's Federation in 1901[12] and the following year the *New Zealand Farmer* published his prizewinning essay on vineyard management.[13] Photographs showed a close-up of impressive grape bunches in his vineyard and a large party of visiting members of parliament devouring them.

Jackman was decades ahead of his time. In answer to questions at the end of his winemaking paper he confirmed that while others relied on the coarse American grape Isabella (forerunner of Albany Suprise) he grew the European classics, Cabernet Sauvignon and the Pinot varieties, and Chasselas, Riesling and Shiraz. And while others depended on added sugar in their winemaking, he avoided it, except in cold wet seasons. In his own words, when his customers at first reacted against dry wines, they were "educated up to them."

In the essay that took the New Zealand Literary and Historical Association's prize he called upon the Department of Agriculture to import phylloxera-resistant rootstocks — a plea soon to be sadly justified. And he advocated the use of bonedust. "I strongly recommend. . .bonedust," he wrote in the essay. It was to be broadcast at the rate of three to five hundredweight an acre. The picture is an appealing one: the winegrower marching up and down his rows, a full bag slung at his chest, two hands plunging in and flinging handfuls to the wind. As events developed a pity there is no photograph.

In 1901 Romeo Bragato was brought back to New Zealand and accepted the new post of government viticulturist. In speeches and reports it was Heathcote Jackman he held up as an example to the country. A special train ran to a field-day at Wairangi (now Te Kauwhata) experimental station in March 1902 and speaking to fruitgrowers from throughout the province Bragato singled out the Heathcote vineyard. "He had visited different parts of the colony," he said, "and his opinion was that they would be justified in spending hundreds of thousands in planting vines. "He had tasted wine, that of Mr Jackman in the Kaipara, equal, and very likely superior, to any wine imported into the country. (Applause.)"[14]

Interviewed in June, Bragato named Jackman's wine as equal to the government's Wairangi vintage. In October he said that Otamatea County was one of the most promising districts in the Auckland province. Jackman's "excellent wines, both white and red. . .were a positive proof of the suitability of both soil and climate for the making of choice light wines of dry quality." They compared favourably with the best wines of the same character on the Continent. Following Bragato's recommendation, the Department of Agriculture began preparing 45 acres for viticulture on the newly established Bickerstaffe experimental farm at the head of the Pahi River.

And then the phylloxera cloud burst over Jackman. His vines became heavily infested. They had to be torn out and the soil sterilized. He had to set about replanting the whole vineyard with grape cuttings grafted on resistant rootstock. And sometime in this saga of triumph and disaster Jackman had special recourse to bonedust. He broke into the Ngati Whatua mausoleum and ground the bones for his vineyard. Whether he crushed them in a hand mill or sent them to Colbeck's flour mill at Batley, where animal bones sometimes alternated with wheat, is not recorded.

Pakeha settlers throughout New Zealand raided burial sites to obtain bone fertilizer. In Auckland, Bycroft's mill above Windmill Road, Mt Eden, ground Ngati Whatua bones from nearby lava caves when the biscuit trade was slack. The British plundered their own battlegrounds on the Continent for the same purpose.[15] But in or out of the context of the times, Jackman's was a horrifying act. The Maori people descended on the mausoleum and demolished it but the precise circumstances have not been established. Perhaps Gittos

Heathcote Jackman (with pipe), Gerald McMurdo, son of a neighbouring grapegrower, and Jackman's son Guy, on the bottling machine.

simply returned to deconsecrate the ground. With his gum buying, wine selling and generous credit at the general store, Jackman remained a central figure in the economy. The painful business was brushed under the mat — where it remains today — and in the eyes of "the Englishmen tribe" Jackman's mana appears not to have diminished.

By 1909 Jackman had five acres replanted in young vines producing 1500 gallons. But the vineyard stagnated and a departmental census in 1913 showed wine production remaining at the same figure. That year Jackman fell ill. He was forced to retire as county chairman and the vineyard went into decline. The oldest son, Ernest, had taken up a Bickerstaffe lease, George fought at Gallipoli, caught enteric fever and came back with a damaged heart, Eric was still a boy; only Guy was available to run the general store and act as caretaker and lamp-lighter on the wharf. Wine press, corking machine and barrels were sold to the Silich family across the water and vintage reverted to the traditional small-scale affair of naked winemakers tramping the grapes with their feet.[16]

Before this end to an era (and the absurdly inflated viticultural bubble had burst everywhere and a discredited Bragato had left the country) Jackman had risen to other heights and again been plunged to the depths. If mission Maoris bore no grudges, did the ancestors keep alive the spirit of utu he had once talked about?

Dreams of the Kaipara's mineral wealth had long been in the back of his mind and in 1906 he set about realizing them. Copper had been found by the

Family group at Heathcote.

earliest settlers and Thomas Coates, for one, had sent samples for analysis with a favourable result, as he told the first meeting of the Kaipara Progress Committee in 1873. Jackman and John Chadwick were the Pahi representatives. The superintendent of the province was petitioned to prospect the district but no action was taken.

Thirty-three years on and Jackman picked up the task personally. He employed Robert Creaghe, a mining expert, to investigate the Kaipara's copper riches. Of the samples sent for analysis from six locations, two "in native or metallic form" were reported to have commercial value. Creaghe's favourable report was backed by an exciting map. It was large and handcoloured and marked by five red parallel lines running through the district, each bearing in red capitals the magic words, COPPER LODE. The lines started at the Oruawharo River and one ended at Matakohe, one ran through Jackman's property to Pahi, another ended at Percy Gibson's farm below Pukehuia and two more reached towards Paparoa. Various blocks of land were picked out in colour, clues to location were provided, the lettering was persuasively professional. Drawn on linen and folded, it opened up like a treasure map.[17]

With W.H. Jackman as chairman, his son Guy secretary, and one of the directors, Percy Gibson, guaranteeing a bank overdraft, the Kaipara Copper Developing Syndicate began negotiating mining rights over large areas. At first a licence was obtained "to enter and mine for copper and other minerals except coal" along the foreshore of the Otamatea and Arapaoa Rivers and then the search moved inland. Gilbert King granted a 99-year mining lease over the Hokorako block, the Dobson Paikea family and Pairama Mu leased the Otamatea block, Parateme Hemana the Opekapeka block — and this was only a start.

The timing was right, particularly for Maori landowners. Fish canning at Batley, almost the only source of employment in the area, was under siege. Sharks were savaging the mullet nets, the harbour was over-fished, and to those perennial worries was added, in 1906, a panic consumer resistance to tinned food. Remarkably, this was the long-distance effect of a book on the Chicago meat industry by a crusading American. Betraying rare bureaucratic emotion, the Department of Agriculture had this to say about the phenomenon:

> Early in the year the canned goods trade received a great shock by the publication of a socialistic book entitled *The Jungle* by Mr Upton Sinclair, exposing the filthy methods in vogue at the Chicago packing-houses. This led to the paralysing of everything packed in tins, and so far did the popular prejudice extend that even biscuits and baking-powder packed in tins were affected by the scare. Although there was much truth in the book, there was also an immense amount of exaggeration, and much that was graphically described therein would sound 'very dreadful' to the layman (especially to ladies), but to those in the trade not so unsatisfactory.[18]

If the power of the printed word could halt an industry on the other side of the world, so it could puff up one close at hand. The weekly *New Zealand Graphic* published a photograph of Otamatea River with a caption reporting that lumps of copper were to be found lying on its beaches, the *Sydney Morning Herald* reported that copper was being mined on the Kaipara and — heady moment —

the Port Kembla Refining Works wrote to Whakapirau asking to buy the ore. The syndicate's extraction machinery was no more than expensive pictures in overseas catalogues — indeed, it had no sampling drill — but self-styled mining experts were practically queuing with propositions to tap untold mine investment money in America and Britain.

Reflecting the general euphoria, a meeting of the Maori owners of six blocks agreed to take shares in lieu of rent for their land. Each block took thirty £1 shares, as did the Pakeha farmer, Gilbert King, who invested his own money in shares as well. A letter from Andrew Wiapo, licensed interpreter, told Jackman of the preparations that had gone into the Maori landowners' meeting:

> Now Mr Jackman, we wish to have a spree here next Saturday on behalf of the copper development in Otamatea. We intend to have supper and conclude with a dance. . ..The idea is to encourage our Maori friends to have an interest of feelings towards their industry and to bring them to the more understanding to this great work and also to encourage their fellow workers to push on with the prospecting system, etc. Billy Paikea will tell you all about it. . .

Jackman himself had always been a convivial host. Bishop Selwyn had been entertained at Heathcote, Seddon had called more that once, the officers on timber ships were welcome (one party had compared his first red wine with French claret — even though made from Isabella) Now the general store buzzed with mining talk. Even morning customers sipped wine and stayed on to savour the excitement. Edith Jackman was reconciled to the noon-day sight of a dozen or more people trailing around the hillside track that bordered the sea below her window. It connected store with house whatever the tide and her husband was bringing some more enthusiasts home for lunch.

By July 1908 when the share register closed some sixty people had put money into the syndicate. Whakapirau millhands, a ploughman, the Pahi policeman, a local doctor, the county clerk, housewives and farmers — the net was cast wide with farmers in the majority and £5 shares the most popular. Even the viticulturist Romeo Bragato, in eclipse as an expert but enthusiasms undimmed, took a £5 share. Gittos had once said there was only one half-crown in Otamatea County but Constable Jonas Abrams had found eight half-crown instalments to pay for his £1 share.

W.H. Jackman, who became county chairman at the height of it all, invested £11, his brother Frank £10 and son Guy £8. Among the bigger investors were J. Ryan, the Pahi publican, £25; Mander and Bradley, sawmillers, £25; J.R. Ross, Whakapirau engineer, £30; A.E. Harding, a Mangawhare farmer (and a director) £30; and J.M. Metcalfe, Hukatere farmer, £40. These were substantial sums and altogether over £500 was raised.

Prospects did not seem so dazzling away from the Kaipara. The general manager of the National Bank wrote in confidence from Wellington to report on the 100 shares he had tried to place, "I am sorry to say so far I have only placed 25 and 20 of these are taken by myself. My friends here are largely in Talismans. . ." And that company's poor outlook had "rather damped their ardour for mining." Perhaps the government's refusal to give a subsidy — it offered instead only free testing of samples at the Thames School of Mines — was seen as showing a lack of confidence. And there was. The Minister of Mines wrote to Francis Mander MP: 'I regret to inform you that reports already obtained in this locality do not at present warrant the expenditure of public money as requested."

Creaghe did not have the same diffidence about private money. He now planned to put the Kaipara on the investment map in America. The bank manager advised Jackman not to accept these plans. He also opposed Creaghe's proposal to buy a diamond drill instead of hiring a government one. A thousand pounds could be saved by hiring, he wrote, and the basis of Creaghe's opposition, "That the man in charge will know too much,' is absurd. What harm can they do? If the result of boring proves a rich field and it becomes known through them, it can only be to the shareholders' advantage."

In a world where jackals at the edges of mining made more than the miners, perhaps Creaghe was after a commission on the sale of a drill. It was also a world where jackal ate jackal. Soon Creaghe's shortcomings were being highlighted from another quarter. Jackman had appointed Quentin Addison McConnell, civil and mining engineer (to quote the letterhead) as engineer to the project and he set about taking over. "With Creaghe in sole control," he wrote to Jackman, "I am now a fifth wheel to a wagon." McConnell ridiculed Creaghe's latest scheme, to travel to London to float a £40,000 company:

> Allow me to advise, 'listen not to the voice of the Charmer, charm he never so sweetly.' You are only deceiving yourselves if you think you can get a big price in London for the Property at present and Mr Creaghe's millions is either only a figurative term or the result of a very vivid imagination.

Jackman had also appointed an agent, W.G. Layly Alexander, to negotiate leases over likely copper-bearing land. In another letter McConnell wrote to Jackman, "to put you on your guard." The agent, he said, "has been showing your letter in several public houses in town. . .the trouble is Alexander takes too much to drink." Also, he was "deeply in debt." A few months later he reported that "Creaghe and Alexander are working together." All very bewildering, particularly as other agents were trying to snap up mining rights on adjoining land. One Cleghorn was said to have signed up 5,000 acres of Maori land around the Otamatea and this put additional pressure on the syndicate to carry out expensive surveys to establish its own boundaries.

In February 1909 Alexander resigned, promising to have no further contact with Maori landowners and ending his letter, "I give you my word I will not interfere with your leases." In August Creaghe was paid off by the syndicate's lawyers, Parr and Blomfield. Advising Jackman of this, C.S. Blomfield wrote that he assumed no shares had been given to Creaghe. If they had, "cancel any shares as made in error." A hundred £1 shares had indeed been placed in the name of Robert Persse Creaghe and that page in the register of shareholders was duly crossed out in red ink with the words "Cancelled — issued without authority of the Directors."

By October, Parr and Blomfield themselves were growing restless. The company's affairs had been amateurishly conducted and they had shepherded it along with reams of advice — advice often ignored. Payment of legal fees had been postponed awaiting mining income — it had been difficult enough to meet survey and legal costs and disbursements to the mining experts — but all the

Chadwick's mill in its hey-day, ss *Melbourne* ready to load. At rear is Guy Jackman's house.

capital raising schemes of Creaghe, Alexander, McConnell, et al, had come to nothing. C.S. Blomfield wrote to Jackman about his account:

> Although the amount owing appears a very large one we have cut down every item as much as we possibly could. The amount of work done was enormous. You will note that the expenses out of pocket were very considerable. We have, however, managed to save you nearly Twenty Pounds in interpreter's fees alone.

That month a restructured company had made a call for further shares. Half the original shareholders failed to respond, but some had not lost their optimism. On the contrary. The Jackman family put in another £40 and co-director, Percy Gibson, added £50 to his original £15. A future Minister of Finance, Gordon Coates, added £20 to his first £6 and took over the bank overdraft guarantee while Gibson made a holiday visit to England. (Rodney Coates was content to rest with his original £5.) Some other additional investments, the original shareholding in brackets, were: Ernest Adams, £25 (£15); D.U. Duthie, bank manager £30 (12); F. Chadwick, mill manager £10 (£5); J. Grieves, ploughman £3 (£2). W.H.Stevens, retired on the Pahi River for thirteen years, but still a comparatively young man, raised his £10 investment by a block-busting £139 — more than a third of the total sum raised. This time contributions outside the Kaipara were again noticeably absent. After three years of sound and fury there were not enough funds even to test drill for mining sites — assuming they existed. And that assumption was one becoming increasingly dubious to make.

As the year ended several began off-loading their shares. Guy Jackman transferred two shares to the local assistant postmistress, two to her sister, four to a local farmer. The Winsers, Whakapirau farmers, succeeded in quitting one share to an Auckland doctor, eight to a Waiuku labourer, and surprisingly far afield, seven to Edmund Clifton of Wellington, the Department of Agriculture's

71

Whakapirau Church, opened 1898.

Director of Experimental Farms. He must have been wrapped in experiments.

Blinded by greed, or perhaps just not very bright — after all, he paid for a parcel of shares in addition to the fifty he was given free — Quentin Addison McConnell could not read the signs. In February 1910 he attempted to prod W.H. Jackman into new activity:

> What is to be done with the Kaipara copper? Surely we must not go to sleep, I say form it into a company of £15,000 with £5,000 Working Capital and start a Diamond drill. I am sure this the proper and only course.

In April he had a fresh proposal. Burton, the managing director of the Silverstream mine, was "striking it rich" and was off to England for money. His syndicate would buy into copper and for "my Kaipara friends" there was "a good chance of big profit with small risk."

The epitaph of the copper bonanza of the Kaipara was written a month later. The company was faced with prosecution for failing to file returns. On 1 June 1910, C.S. Blomfield wrote to tell Jackman that the prosecution had been withdrawn when he had paid the two guinea fee required out of his own pocket. "When," the lawyer asked, "can I expect remittance as promised?"

William Heathcote Jackman could not meet his outstanding debts. The copper fiasco had left him, in effect, bankrupt. There were other blows. Trade at the general store had fallen away with the close-down of Chadwick's mill after a fire. He had been generous with credit for Maori and other customers but with no mining employment or dividends, bad debts totalling £1000 had to be written off. And the Auckland warehouse holding a shipment of kauri gum ready for export burned down. The shipment was uninsured. (Earlier the top floor of Heathcote itself was gutted — not mysteriously, for brother Frank had an unsteady hand in this disaster.)

72

An Anglican lay preacher, Heathcote Jackman had rich experiences to draw on when he delivered a sermon to mark the end of the first world war. He spoke of those who "puffed up with their own conceit. . .forgot the Almighty Ruler of the Universe and his Teaching" and sharing his homespun philosophy with the Whakapirau congregation, went on to say:

> . . .remember that there is no such thing as stopping still either in business or religion, you must be either moving ahead or moving back. Will each person here ask himself or herself this question 'Am I a better man or woman than I was a year ago?' or rather 'Is the world better during the last year through any exertions of mine?' You must realize when you look around you and see the life of men, animals and plants, that there must be a Supreme Ruler. Even in our puny way a household or a business must have a head. . .[19]

Son Guy shouldered the debts of the Jackman household and it was twenty years after his father's death in 1923 (at the age of 77) before he finally cleared them. The amiable Frank, sent out to live under his brother's care, survived him by fifteen years. His mother, a deeply religious woman who left a large part of her fortune to the church, had tied up enough of it invested in London Counties stock to keep her son at Whakapirau in comfort and in drinking money all his long life. He died at 84 in 1938.

The scene of so much Kaipara history is now hidden in trees behind an oyster farm. A cellar building, still leaning drunkenly in 1976, a few vat hoops rusting on the earth floor, has since collapsed and disappeared. And the last remaining vine, then a thick trunk straggling up a tree, has died. But Heathcote stands, roof lowered to a single storey after the fire of long ago. It has been brought back into family ownership and is being restored by a great grandson. Behind the house and alongside the old vineyard area, a pa site is to be preserved. No doubt worthless lumps of copper will continue to be found, "small segregations of native copper," in the words of a DSIR geology bulletin, "which led to some abortive prospecting in times past."

Cellar relics, 1976.

Lionel de Labrosse and his first house at the head of Pahi River.

Chateau de Varennes, the family seat.

5. *The count who ate with the crew*

DEATH NOTICE
de Labrosse, at her daughter's residence, Eversleigh,
Remuera, Jane Isabella, widow of the late Viscomte
de Labrosse of Varennes, Nantes and Pahi, Kaipara.
— *Herald*, 27/1/1917

Viscomte Lionel James Edgard Rousseau de Labrosse, a resonant name. None more distinguished has been transplanted from the old world to Pahi or, for that matter, to Remuera. The count, his Anglo-Irish wife Jane Isabella and infant son John Edgard Lucien, arrived in Auckland en route to Pahi on the sailing ship *Regina* on 10 March 1867. They brought with them £1000, twelve silver teaspoons, and an impeccable royalist pedigree.[1]

A ship named *Regina*, reigning queen, may have stirred unhappy memories on the voyage out for a man whose last queen, Marie Antoinette, had gone under the guillotine (and whose grandfather and great grandmother had perished with her in the same revolution) but the silver spoon heirlooms — exquisitely tooled and refined to the point of fragility — were tangible reassurance of past glories.[2] If hardships and hunger became intolerable in the bush at Pahi they could always eat cake with them.

The de Labrosse family seat was Chateau de Varennes, near Angers, Main-et-Loire. And here, at the head of the rich Loire valley, the family had established centuries of feudal credentials in the service of French kings. How far back, it is not possible to trace for as *Archives Historiques,* Paris, records: "The Rousseau de Labrosse family, pursued like all the existing noble families by the revolution of 1789, had all their estates sequestered and sold by the nation, all documents and titles burned by the vandals of the period. Owing to these losses, this family can authentically trace back their direct line only as far as 1570."[3]

For Lionel de Labrosse, 25 years old when he stepped ashore on the shell beach at Pahi, the nine generations to 1570 was perhaps baggage enough. Certainly the labels were impressive: Michel Rousseau, lord of Rimogne de Labrosse and earldom of Hiraumont, corp commander of Henry of Navarre's troops at the battle of Evy, 1590 . . . Gui de Labrosse, scientist and doctor to Louis XIII whose bust in white marble commemorates his founding of the Paris zoological gardens, 1625 . . . Pierre de Labrosse, colonel in Louis XIV's army killed at the crossing of the Rhine, 1672 . . . Charles de Labrosse, captain of the guards, killed by the first shots of the English at Fontenoy, 1745 . . .

On the maternal side Francois Jaunay, lieutenant-general in the artillery corps of Louis XV, fought the Duke of Marlborough in the famous battle of Malplaquet, 1709. So distinguished were this ancestor's feats of arms in the German wars, in Flanders and in Spain that letters patent granted by the king at Versailles in 1726 conferred on him the truly exceptional right to pass on his titles to his only child — a daughter.

Archives Historiques records the fate of this woman, Lionel de Labrosse's great grandmother, and that of her son and grandson in these (abbreviated) words:

> Madam Rousseau de Labrosse was a widow at the time when the first Revolution reached the climax of its violence. She was denounced by the revolutionary committee of Angers as being a royalist and, with several other ladies of the first noble families, was taken on foot to Paris. As a result of the hardships undergone she died in the cathedral of Chartres which had been converted into a prison.

> Joseph Vincent Rousseau de Labrosse [Lionel's grandfather] was a friend of the celebrated la Perouse and accompanied him on one of his voyages round the world. Ruined and pursued by the revolutionaries, he joined the army of Charette, finding thus the opportunity of avenging his mother's sufferings and death as well as serving the king's cause. Wounded in 1794 he succumbed two years later to the after effects of his wounds.

> Joseph Lucien Rousseau de Labrosse [Lionel's father] born 1795, was the head of the family. He became a cavalry lieutenant on the emperor Napoleon's return from the isle of Elba, campaigned in Belgium and was wounded during the sad day of Waterloo. He was later imprisoned for having fought a duel with officers of the new royal guards, and in 1825 withdrew to his estate, the Chateau de Varennes. He was a commanding officer of troops during the insurrection of 1852.

Joseph de Labrosse married an Englishwoman, a Protestant, Sophie Tyrell, daughter of a captain in the Royal Navy. It was not a match to recoup the family fortunes. Impoverished noble houses were as ruthless with younger sons as they had been with serfs and for Lionel de Labrosse, their second son, his only patrimony a set of spoons (the £1000 was almost certainly his wife's

Lionel and Jane de Labrosse and their first child, photographed before migrating.

dowry) any claim to landed estates shrank to claiming a free grant in New Zealand — 40 acres for himself and 40 acres for his wife.

The grant, next to Greenhills, 750 acres bought by his wife's affluent brother, Robert Hill, was in the upper reaches of Pahi River opposite the rock, Tokatapu. It offered daunting bush, niggardly soil and remote tidal waters. After the sweet Loire, a salt river.

Thomas Cockayne stood on an adjoining grant on Christmas Day, 1862, and remembering many happy Christmas Days in England, had written home to declare he "never felt so well, happy and thankful to God on this day."[4] Described in *The Albertlanders* as "the first white woman to land at Pahi," his wife might equally well have been described as the first to leave. Both the Cockaynes and a neighbour, J. Martin, abandoned their forty acres after a year. Further up the river, the Metcalfe family gave it six months over the summer 1863-64 and shifted to Clairmont on the Arapaoa. In de Labrosse's first year he saw John Chadwick forsake his claim (and quit his gum-buying store) to move down to Pahi. Some came, took one look, and didn't bother trying. Lionel and Jane de Labrosse stayed for eight years.

Unlike most settlers, they had capital to draw on — £1000 was a large sum at that time — and while waiting at the Pahi "barracks", now George Haines's boarding house, they had a substantial house built back from the water. Even a small church was erected by the river landing where the Wesleyan missionary James Buller conducted a service in 1875 and baptized one of the children. "The worshippers came in boats and filled the building," he later wrote.[5]

If the estate was minuscule, it was at least splendidly sited. It was on a tongue of land surrounded on three sides by the twisting river — the first loop in a series of S-bends that had given the upper reaches of the tideway the name Whakatakawai, the water that turns and takes a circuitous course. And those waters were teeming with fish, the bush thick with weka, wood pigeon and wild pig — a good place for de Labrosse to exercise his only skill: hunting, shooting and fishing.

A daughter had been born ten days after the family arrived in New Zealand and in the years at Tokatapu three more daughters and a second son were born. The arrival of "Captain" Colbeck on a great land buying spree offered an opportunity to move the family closer to essential services. Colbeck bought Hill's adjoining block in 1877 and in amassing 18,000 acres every 40 acres counted, particularly as he coveted the Labrosse grant as the site for his own headquarters.

The family's new location, just down river from the boatyard, builder's workshop and smithy of W.J. Symonds, was on elevated ground so close to civilization that Pahi itself could be seen. On a promontory with sweeping views of the harbour, a trading schooner at anchor below, life could take on some of the colour that romantic illusion gave the South Pacific. De Labrosse bought such a schooner and planned to trade on the Kaipara. On its maiden voyage the ship was wrecked, the mate drowned, and the owner was lucky to escape with his life.[6]

An early view of Pahi showing the mill before it moved to Whakapirau.

The cutter *Pai Marire* in Matakohe River, 1870, with Metcalfe's Clairmont on the skyline. From John Backhouse's sketchbook.

De Labrosse had adapted well to manual skills and turned to gumdigging, boat building, carpentry, and at Symond's mill operated a stationary steam engine. At one stage he contracted to carry mail between Pahi and Dargaville and he even seems to have run a water taxi (the Linnell diaries record that he ferried a passenger by yacht up the Otamatea).[7] He shared an interest with the Linnell's in the schooner *Sea Breeze* and on one memorable voyage to the Aratapu sawmills for timber it came close to sharing the fate of his first vessel. "On this expedition," the Linnells record, "the pilot Heta Paikea was the worse for liquor most of the time and the ship and cargo were fortunate to get home intact."

At least de Labrosse craft performed well at regattas. In the sailing event of 1877, for instance, his yacht *Dolly Varden* came second, as did his punt *Kaipara Barge*, in the rowing event. (Incidentally, if the Paikea competing at the same regatta was the pilot Heta Paikea, then his hand was not always unsteady — he came second in the egg-and-spoon race.)

Although their capital had been whittled away the family contrived elegance on a shoe-string. Parcels of clothing came from France so that the de Labrosse turn-out at local functions was a spectacle of white gloves, tails and well cut gowns. And often enough in the earliest days it was their piano, transported athwart a dinghy, that provided the music.

Their house was a marvel of style with economy. The living room, coved ceiling, french doors to a northerly verandah, an end bay window to the water, was perfectly proportioned. So pleasing are the lines of this room (preserved unchanged today) that it comes as a surprise to discover that the interior walls are unlined. Pit-sawn kauri vertical weatherboards are the only cladding and the sturdy studs are so well spaced and carefully bevelled that their presence enhances the architecture. Whether the common practice was followed of pasting unlined walls with the pages of illustrated magazines to keep out the draught, it is not possible to say.[8]

It has been said in the family that de Labrosse spoke in broken English. Strongly accented seems more likely, because three of his surviving letters indicate good — and for the times even superior — command of the language. They also betray a highly developed sense of distance from the working class whose ranks he had compulsorily joined. Adversity bred no fellow-feeling and the incongruity of this situation did not escape local people. They generally referred to him, in a certain tone of voice, as "the *count*". The West family, with its sturdy Quaker levelling attitudes, has preserved the memory of one socially lethal incident when de Labrosse was working for Arthur Forrester, the Whakapirau boat builder, on a visiting sailing ship. They were caulking its timbers. Inviting Forrester to his cabin for lunch, the captain said; "Your man can go for'ard."[9]

In the official record of freeholders in 1882 he is listed as owning 25 acres at Te Pahi, value, £350. Occupation, "Master Mariner." But the reality was that the depression of the '80s made even casual labouring work hard to find. Forced to travel outside the district, de Labrosse ended up at the Chelsea sugar works. In nineteenth century New Zealand he could not have found a more savage industrial hell-hole. A letter to his daughter, Ada Louisa, written in May 1889 does not disguise his misery:

> I must write a few lines . . . to ask your forgiveness for not writing sooner but if you knew what work we have been doing since I returned. Day and night I have been here nearly all the time returning to the works at 2 and three in the morning loading and back at eight o'clock unloading, twice a week. I spent my last Sunday with them. I leave on Friday for my new place . . .

Of that prospect, setting up a bush sawmill at Wairakau, near Te Aroha, he was not hopeful. "Write as often as you can for it will be my only pleasure to hear from you all in my desolate swamp with nothing but Maoris to speak to." Perhaps, given time, they could have swapped genealogies. But after 22 years in New Zealand the common touch had eluded him. Three weeks later, on June 1, he wrote to his sister-in-law, Mrs Elizabeth Hill:

> Both my bosses left for Te Aroha after lunch so I am all alone in the desert. We began work in earnest last Thursday with a gang of Maoris. I protested about it but the Bosses would not listen. The consequence was that today at 11 o'clock they struck work and had to be sacked. I was rather pleased . . .

He shared a bush hut with his Pakeha employers — and cooked for them — but their company was hardly more appealing. Both were "about as useless men as ever went in for mill work. . .life in this Commonwealth is not to my liking," he wrote, and looked forward to building his own quarters. Nature, rather than humanity, pleased his eye, particularly Te Aroha mountain, ". . .half always in clouds it is really a grand sight. Just in front of our Shanty there is a waterfall about a 1000 ft above us and at the distance it must be 300 ft of a strait face. We can hear it and see the wind blowing the spray away. I thought I should feel very lonely this evening but I dont."

A week later he again wrote to his daughter, Ada Louisa. If her status had improved (she had married a retired sea captain who had purchased Maramarua, a large block near Whakapirau) his life was no easier with the replacement of Maori labour by a Pakeha work force.

> We have had strikes here already having to employ the most fearful larakins and Demons ever heard of. Nearly every day we have had to sack some. We keep a very strict discipline or else I would not manage them. I am glad to hear your Servants are giving you satisfaction. . . There are no nice people about and very few of any sort except far apart.

He hoped his daughter would visit Te Aroha. "Really the mountains are beautiful. I was out at six this morning to light my fire . . . the lightning was very beautiful playing over the mountain top." And he hoped to spend Christmas with his family in six months' time. "I think I shall get more encouragement than I did at the Refinery and better remuneration. I hope I shall be able to go up at Xmas and have the pleasure of inspecting Maramarua and the inmates of it."[10]

This letter was dated 8 June. In three weeks he was dead. He died at the sawmill on 29 June 1889. There was no doctor in attendance and no medical certificate to give the cause of death. A coroner's jury at Te Aroha delivered a verdict to their own satisfaction: "Died by visitation of God in a natural way."[11] In Te Aroha cemetery a tiny headstone, hardly bigger than a case of silver spoons, marks his grave. The inscription is mostly indecipherable. He was 47.

Jane de Labrosse confronted widowhood with one daughter married, both her sons already adults and the youngest daughter almost 15. A strong personality, Jane was Anglo-Irish with a family history as distinguished in the service of British civil and military occupation forces as her late husband's had been in the service of the French crown. Not as dashing, but every bit as bloody.

Jane's mother was a Reilly of Scarvagh and the Reilly's, discarding the Irish prefix O', had founded their fortune by making presents of fresh eggs, cherries and other fruits to William of Orange on the eve of the Battle of the Boyne. The Dutch mercenary had rewarded Jane's ancestors with a grant of land as large as he could walk around in a day.[12] Jane's father, the Rev John Hill, was vicar of Donaghdee, County Down — a post in Northern Ireland not at odds with the behaviour of the Reilly's.

Jane had met her husband when he was in Ireland visiting a sister who had married a British army officer. He was 21 and she was some years older when she married him in the family mansion, Scarvagh House, where her great-uncle

Jane Isabella de Labrosse.

stored drums and banners for the annual re-enactment of the Boyne on its sloping meadows.

It was her connections that led them to the Kaipara. Francis Hull, son of an Irish linen millowner at Donaghdee, had left for New Zealand in 1860 to settle up the Otamatea River. In 1866 Jane's two brothers, Robert and William Hill, with their friends Nicholas Martin and William Stoney, were preparing for the Kaipara too, when the de Labrosse newly-weds returned to Ireland from a stay in Algiers with another of Lionel's sisters, Baroness de Merthens. With their infant son, they joined the expedition.

The ship called at Capetown where a whaling fleet was about to leave for the Antarctic. Lionel de Labrosse was powerfully drawn. The family history notes: "It became necessary for Madam de Labrosse, who was expecting her second child, to exert some pressure to convince her husband that whaling was not his forte and that his first duty was to his wife and child, and that they should all proceed with the ship." Whether adventure or escape was his motivation is not recorded.

It says something of Jane de Labrosse's strength of will that, in Victorian times, her associations and not her husband's, were drawn upon to name their Pahi house. It was called Cloon Even after the house of a maternal ancestor, a grand-daughter of Viscount Bangor.[13]

Cloon Even had seen one daughter married at 22 to retired master mariner Captain Percy Haggerston Gibson (someone with the wealth, as we have seen, to provide servants) but such eligible bachelors were not plentiful on the Kaipara. Nine years later, in 1897, Cloon Even toasted the marriage of 28-year-old Mary Augusta to Percy Waterfield Shakespear of Pahi, gentleman — and recipient of a regular income from overseas. The rough democracy of colonial

New Zealand that served so harsh a fate on a French count had worse in store for an English gentleman.

"One sees very distinctly in Thackeray's style, as in his way of thinking and feeling about things, the English public school and university man — the tone of one born and bred to be a gentleman." So a Victorian critic approvingly described the novelist, William Makepeace Thackeray. Of that style he added, "We may also see it in a certain conversational ease and grace . . . the direct opposite of the detestable style . . . of so many inferior men."[14]

How Percy Shakespear, remittance man, faithful customer of the Pahi hotel — and Thackeray's cousin — regarded the conversational standards in the bar is not on record. But certainly he did not let them keep him away. Among the flotsam washed up in that place of solace he was one with a more-than-ordinary sense of inadequacy to drown. His mother was Thackeray's aunt, his father, John Talbot Shakespear, was a high panjandrum of empire in the Bengal Civil Service. His younger brother — *younger* brother — became General Sir Richmond Shakespear, a born-and-bred ruler of India, his older brother Colonel John Shakespear, was the model for Colonel Newcome, a "noble and kindly" hero of Thackeray's celebrated novel *The Newcomes*.[15]

Percy let it be known that rejection by the Indian Army had led him to the Kaipara. A rejection, it seemed, not due to deficiencies in horsemanship. Shakespear could ride, and no matter his condition or the hour of night, simply spurred his horse in the inky direction of home — and clung on. The well-worn route included the hurdling of a slip-rail gate.

The Shakespear fortunes seemed to rise with a marriage to the daughter of the late Count Lionel de Labrosse. A son, Lionel Percy, was born the following year. Perhaps these events excessively revived the ease and grace of his conversational tones in the bar. Whatever the reason, his drinking companions thought it amusing to add another rail to the gate.[16]

The horse came down in the dark and the rider died. He was 32 years old. A premonition, despair, simply another bar-room joke? — whatever the cause, remittance funds had gone to pre-ordering a plot in the Pahi cemetery, £1/10/- paid in 1896.[17] Percy Shakespear was buried in his plot the first week of March, 1898, and the headstone, a handsome marble cross, is the only stone standing in what is now an overgrown and cattle-trodden graveyard.

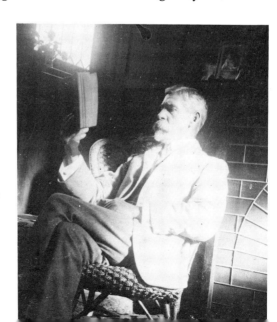

Percy Gibson.

Tyrell de Labrosse and his sisters Ada and Violet.

The newly-born heir lived for ten months and died in 1899. Shakespear's widow later married a British army officer and lived in England until returning to New Zealand in old age to live with her sister, Mrs Percy Gibson.

Violet Helen, the third daughter, married Douglas Cromwell Snelling of Maungaturoto, farmer, Boer War veteran and leader of a group of mounted specials who rode to Auckland to break the 1913 waterfront strike.[18] The long arm of Irish history again touched the Kaipara with this match. The bride's forebears, as has been noted, gave comfort to William of Orange; the bridegroom's middle name reflected a direct line of descent from one who had left an equally heavy imprint on Ireland — Oliver Cromwell.[19] From this marriage seven children were born, their descendants farming in the region today.

Augusta Caroline, the fourth daughter , married George Linnell in 1898 and lived on the Linnell family farm, Te Ihu, on the Otamatea. Not for the youngest de Labrosse the finery from France. She wore a riding habit at her wedding, the first held in the new Whakapirau church, and bride and bridegroom rode to their home by swimming the horses across the river behind a rowboat manned by the groom's two sisters. Six children were born and two of the three boys were given de Labrosse as a second Christian name. It reappeared in the next generation as a grand-daughter's name but there was now no royal hand at Versailles to decree a female line of descent when the male line ran out — as it did when the de Labrosse brothers both died young.

Lionel de Labrosse's ill-fortune was visited on his sons. The oldest John Edgard Lucien, died of pneumonia in 1895 while working as a surveyor's assistant at Coromandel. He was only thirty years old. It was left to Tyrell de Labrosse, keen member of the Otamatea Mounted Rifles, to uphold the military traditions of his family. He enlisted for the Boer War, served as an NCO in the short, sharp campaigning of the 8th contingent and steamed for home with a thousand soldiers on the *Britannic*.

Bedding was lice infested, many had no change of underclothing and, in crowded, poorly ventilated sleeping quarters, hammocks were slung on hooks 18 inches (46 cm) apart. Rather than endure these conditions many troops slept on mess tables and open decks. An epidemic of measles and pneumonia swept the ship and twenty died during the voyage or after landing, in quarantine on Somes Island. Corporal Tyrell Lionel Lushington de Labrosse was buried at sea. He was 31. In terms of the glorious martial deaths of his French ancestors, history again had repeated itself, first as tragedy and then as farce.

And farcical were the findings of an official inquiry headed by Sir William Russell Russell, Sandhurst born and educated, who had escaped active service in the Anglo-Maori wars by selling his commission to become a Hawkes Bay squatter. A port health officer reported that the ship's hospital was overcrowded and dirty and it was established that hospital orderlies were disembarked in Wellington the day before shore treatment was organized. The sick and dying were left without nursing through the night and had to depend on help from a few volunteers. The commission of inquiry found the army free of blame.[20]

British soldiers, it seemed, could sleep in hammocks 16 inches (41 cm) apart, the men had spread infection themselves by spitting, some had concealed their high fever in the hope of getting ashore earlier. In reply to evidence of poor food the commission found that apart from "the occasional jar of rhubarb jam that had fermented" the food was good but "no doubt on many occasions the cooking was unsavoury." Tea and coffee boiled in the same coppers as meat and served in greasy soup dixies were "drinkable, although not nice." A joke from *Punch* was quoted to show that on passenger liners fault was sometimes found with the service.

In France the de Labrosse mausoleum has plaques recording the dates when Lionel de Labrosse and his two sons met their end. Chateau de Varennes was occupied by German forces in World War Two — with or without collaboration is unknown. The de Labrosse family has long departed and the chateau is now owned by Americans.[21]

Douglas Cromwell Snelling, a 1913 special,
from a watersider's pamphlet.

Kohi Pook with her eighteenth baby, Vance. At rear are Tosti and Tom, both born while she worked the steam launch *Matarere*.

6. *No picnic at Puriri Point*

Oh, friend! send your young men to Tanoa that they may see our maidens, and
may know that they are good for wives.

-Arama Karaka, quoted in *Brighter Britain*

"The Pooks have taken fifty times more fish out of the Kaipara than any other
family . . . Ted Pook lived on the water, he fished seven days a week no matter
the weather . . . Kohi Pook was a fine woman, she was tiny but sat under the big
fig on regatta day accepting tribute like a matriarch when her children took prizes
. . . Mrs Pook was dignified, beautifully spoken, she was always alone, I never
once saw her with her husband — he would always be fishing I suppose . . ."

The story was always the same: the big man and his fierce single-mindedness,
the little woman with the engaging personality and the grace she imparted to the
enormous family she reared.

Edward James Pook and Kohinga Mika Haira barged house and their first six
children from Oneroa Bay on Pouto Peninsula to Puriri Point at Christmas 1926.
Kohi mixed a Christmas cake on the way and cooked it on an open fire when she
landed. Ted anchored a thick rope to a tree and the four oldest children stayed in
the house and pulled themselves ashore. Ted had built a capstan from an upright
length of stout macrocarpa drilled with holes to take two crowbar handles and set
in bearings on the floor and ceiling. The bearings were hollowed wooden blocks,
the bottom one filled with shark oil. The children turned the bars, the rope
wrapped around the trunk and as the house inched forward Ted moved the rope
anchorage back from tree to tree.

The house was long and narrow and sat its full length on two kauri rickers. It
became, in effect, a giant sledge, and it took less than two hours for two boys and
two girls to pull it to high ground. The operation was so effortless — for Pook —
that he recorded it with an old bellows camera, a unique child-labour
documentation lost in the still harder years ahead.[1]

Home for the Pooks was no better than an oversize gumdigger's shanty. Built
of rough-sawn vertical boards, unlined, the windows were sacks rolled up or
down according to the weather. Cooking was by open fire in the bowels of a
corrugated iron chimney, a chimney as large as a room — so large the barge
had to make a separate trip to carry it. Wire hooks dangled from its cavernous
shaft, a collection of camp ovens sat in the ashes and for the fast element an
iron bar bent into a U was balanced on bricks. Day and night in the mosquito
season dried cow dung smouldered as an insecticide. Kerosene tins cut to

The Pook shanty at Oneroa Bay before the move to the Point. Smokehouse at left.

different sizes were the containers, the utensils and the measure for all things. Benzine boxes were the furniture. Bill Pook marvelled as a child at a chest of drawers made by sliding carefully shaped tins in a bank of boxes — a refinement he saw in someone else's house.

Puriri Point, half way between Pahi and the Funnel, was as isolated and lonely as it is today. At the foot of a bush-covered headland it was a strip, just above sea level, where puriri giants threw twisted shadows tracing the outlines of long-abandoned gardens. Shell middens and a few broken adzes brought direct contact with the past. A pocket handkerchief patch cut off from land access, it had escaped the Pakeha land-buyers.[2] Born north of the Kaipara at Kaihu in 1895 and adopted by the chiefly Kena family of Pouto, Kohi had become part-owner of this forlorn fragment by swapping titles to land at even more remote Oneroa Bay.

Ted Pook was born in 1878, four years after his father, a Londoner, came out as a steam engineer for Nicholson's mill at Topuni. Ted gained a river master's ticket on Kaipara steamers and then operated his own launch and barge service. The wife and seven children of a broken marriage were at Dargaville when he fell ill and was bedridden at Pouto. Kohi Haira, a girl of 14 or 15, brought food and nursed him to health. Soon she was towing barges with one steam launch, the *Matarere*, while he ran another, the *Thistle*. It was a grand harbour spectacle when the *Thistle*, its hold spilling over with shells, hoisted a booster sail and on a tow-line to the *Matarere* hauled a chain of shell laden barges for Dargaville footpaths.[3]

The 40-foot *Matarere's* steam engine was powerful but her coal-fired boiler required little stoking — it ran for miles on a sugar bag of coal — a doubly welcome consideration since two babies, first Thomas and then Tosti, were born while Kohi was at the wheel. Only the last two of her nineteen children were delivered in a maternity home. "Take the day off, I don't need you fussing about," Kohi told the Paparoa nurses, as well she might since all her children were successfully reared to adulthood at Puriri Point except for one that was stillborn and one that died in infancy of diptheria.

When the Pooks moved to the Point, Ted had become a full-time fisherman and they were half way through paying off the Logan-built *Arizona*, a 36-footer of 1914 vintage powered by a 20hp petrol engine. It was purchased for £330 on a 100 per cent government fisheries promotion loan, repayable over ten years.[4] Six-monthly payments of £21/3/6 were a struggle — sometimes the full amount had to be made up by borrowing, but on the Kaipara, it is said, the Pooks were the only ones in the depression to pay back the whole debt. Augustus (Bunnie) Tilby of Tinopai who fished in partnership with Pook for several years sold his launch and became a fisheries inspector, the others were insurance write-offs after fires and other convenient mishaps.

With Pook, no Logan craft has ever had quite the same care. He scavenged wrecks at the Heads for big copper bolts, fitted wooden handles, and shaped them into soft hammers for tapping out parts in engine maintenance. He set up sheets of iron sloping to the sun, spread sharks' livers over them, and caught the melting oil in a row of tins at the bottom of the corrugations. The oil was mixed with red lead to give the *Arizona's* paintwork a shine. Shark oil was rubbed unadulterated into the deck and dodger (weather screen) and he kept on applying it until the timbers were saturated. A farmer's wife across the river at Paige Point recalls that it took two or three years to complete the job. "The final finish was beautiful, but for all those years the smell was awful."[5]

She was lucky not to live nearer to Puriri Point for Pook also rendered down rotting livers to make grease for the launch. And to ring-net schools of mullet he packed the rowlocks with grease, tacked greenhide to oiled oars and silently circled the fish. With the help of one of the children in a second boat they were mustered in a tight bunch like a mob of sheep.

Ellen Blackwell visits Puriri Point in 1905 when it was a popular picnic spot.

Ted Pook, literally head and shoulders above fellow crew members on a Kaipara river steamer.

Ted Pook loved his launch and he fished to pay for it and he fished to provide for all the children Kohi bore him. Over 6 foot 2 inches (188cm) tall, there was Dutch blood in his background and he had a plentiful inheritance of that awesome, unrelenting doggedness the Dutch are capable of. His favoured fishing ground was at the Heads, close in to the sand bars where breakers filled the air with permanent spray. He fished there in all conditions, even in raging weather when he had to tie himself to the boat. It was scarred with grooves and rope burns from the fishing lines and the coaming was ringed with indentations — hollows worn in the wood by the pressure of his knees. Oilskins were worn for days on end and the chafing of the salt-wet collar on his jaw — on the left side, the lee side where his head was pressed away from the south-westerlies — was given as the cause of the facial cancer that ultimately killed him.

Pook was as hard on the children as he was on himself. With his oldest boy Tom, even harder. Tom was taken away from the school after primer two and, unbelievably, at seven he was dry setting 600-yard flounder nets single-handed. At that age he began standing-in for his father if he was sick or away rounding up wild horses, hunting pigs or shooting snipe (godwits) on the dunes. He took the *Arizona* to sea in sole command, sometimes fishing with his still younger brother Jack, but mostly he was alone. Memorably, he was head of the family at twelve when Ted and Kohi took the steamer to Dargaville to marry. Divorce from Pook's first wife, a Pakeha, had taken some time.

Pook expected a man's work from his oldest son and he enforced his demands by instant blows or by remote control with fancy cuts from a flicking stockwhip. Mohi Manukau, whose Arapaoa family were the nearest neighbours, once saw young Tom ordered to throw out an anchor. The crosspiece caught in his braces and he was carried overboard. Pook just stood and watched. At the point when Mohi's father — no mean taskmaster himself — was about to intervene, the boy finally fought free and surfaced. It was not an isolated episode. In an age when harsh treatment of children was commonplace, Pook went too far.

At home there was no piped water, no power, no petrol engine — twelve boys and five girls were the energy source. "We depended on the 'Armstrong' patent," says Bill Pook. "If water was needed you carried kerosene tins full in your strong arms — from a spring 250 yards away. For heating and cooking it was the strong arm again — chopping tea tree and mangroves."

For the girls, washing clothes was a hand-rubbing, cold water chore at the spring. Twenty cows were hand-milked by the children in outdoor bails and they rowed the cream to a pick-up point across the harbour before rowing the long haul to school. In winter, knuckles on oars were purple with cold — as were bare feet in the wet bottom of the boat. (Bernice, the youngest daughter, although born to better times, was twelve when she wore her first shoes). A second launch, the *Arawa*, was added to the fishing fleet, but no matter the weather, no launch was available for cream or school.

Kumara was the main crop and Pook sledged tidal mud up behind the house to fertilize the land — a good idea if only a way could have been found to desalinate the mud without losing its rich store of trace elements. But the staple diet was fish and an enormous smokehouse, almost as big as the house chimney, was seldom idle. A neighbour across the harbour remembers Kohi Pook coming every year to buy a wether mutton carcase as a Christmas treat. One year when she threw in the usual lamb with the deal Mrs Pook said: "When the kids have got through this they'll say, 'Where's the fish, mum?'"[6]

The *Arizona* was registered for passenger transport and carried large parties to huis, land court hearings and other Maori gatherings. She was also available for chartered fishing expeditions. Tom Pook recalls trips made by Gordon

Tom Pook on the *Arizona*,
three-years-old and soon
at the wheel.

Coates and a Dargaville lawyer named Hayes — "Bully" Hayes he was called — a man so wide in the beam a special lavatory seat had to be made for him. Every year they spent a week, sometimes longer, cruising the fishing grounds. While his father entertained the paying guests, young Tom ran the launch, shelled oysters, gutted fish, cooked and cleaned. The adults enjoyed a whisky session in the evenings and a long day ended for Tom with the preparation of fish cakes for a 10pm supper. It was a ritual that never varied and Coates, then Prime Minister, rewarded the boy with his first razor. Hayes once gave him a sheath knife.

There was a real diversion when a message arrived at the Point with news that the prophet and healer T.W. Ratana, the Mangai, the mouthpiece, was coming to Tanoa and he would prove his powers by healing the sick. It is a strong boyhood memory for Tom Pook. "'You'd better go and see that,' Dad said to Mum. 'Yes,' she said, 'I'm going all right.'"

Kohi, a Methodist, was not caught up in the bushfire spread of the Ratana movement. Tom and his mother went as sceptical observers. At Tanoa it seemed thousands had gathered. With standing room only in the church the Pooks stood on forms at the back. The Mangai held up a crippled girl. Her limbs were hopelessly twisted and he worked over them with rising intensity. "There was weird talking and strange sounds, his face was shining with sweat — we could see it running off his pointed chin. Then he put the girl down and she walked out of the church. She was still walking the last time I saw her." Tom Pook knew the crippled girl. She was twelve-year-old Janie Harihari from Pouto. Her father was the first Maori in the district to own a motorbike. (Mohi Manukau attended the same service and saw the healing. It was a still day — a piercing out-of-this-world stillness can hang over the Kaipara — and yet Mohi recalls that trees around the church quivered.)[7]

Back home to the not-so-healing lick of the stockwhip another miracle, at least a near-miracle, gave Tom his deliverance from bondage. Fishing at the Heads with eleven-year-old Jack, he was forced to take shelter from an easterly gale. They went ashore near Pouto in time to see a laden boat overturn in the wild sea. It was a surfboat landing supplies from the government lighthouse ship *Matai* and returning the keeper's family after a trip away. Tom kicked off his gumboots and swam out. First he rescued the lightkeepers wife ("Mrs Sinclair was a big woman") and then finding there were others drowning, returned to bring in two children. He helped right the capsized surfboat when it drifted ashore and then slipped away to dry out on the launch.

Weeks later a cheque arrived in the mail, a £20 reward from the Marine Department. "Somehow Dad took a poor view of this. He became more demanding than ever. Next time I sold fish at the lighthouse the keeper suggested I apply for a job on the *Matai*. He had the forms and I let him fill them in. A month later I was accepted." The atmosphere at home grew uglier. "You won't have the guts to go," said Pook. That was a mistake. "If you try to stop me I'll have to report you to the police for assault."

Young Jack took Tom to Pouto to catch the steamer to Helensville. His mother had passed over £12 from the reward. Aged fifteen and the first money in his pocket after years of toil. "That's not much," said Captain Tommy Sellars of the *Ruawai* and pulled out a handful of notes from his wallet. The captain helped him get a train ticket to Wellington — he had never seen a train — and after a bewildering change at Auckland and a rocket journey through the night he was decanted into the streets of the capital. In search of Lyttelton wharf and the light-ship he crossed a road laced with steel tracks. Bells clanged and suddenly trams seemed to bear down from all directions. A boy with a cardboard suitcase had brought traffic to a stop. A policeman came to the rescue. He was a Maori and he carried the suitcase all the way to the ship.

On board Tom was greeted as the hero of the surfboat disaster. "You acted like a man," the captain said, "and on this ship we will treat you like one." He passed a box-the-compass test with ease and the captain turned to the officers: "Some of our ABs can't do that. Teach this man all you know."

At the first pay (£6 a month), Tom was asked for a signature. He didn't know what they were talking about. The discovery of his illiteracy was not spread about. Two officers coached him and while the others slept he learned to read and write. Tom Pook became chief engineer on lighthouse ships and he commanded fisheries patrol vessels. His distinguished war service ranged from sub-Antarctic waters to the tropics. In the battle of the Coral Sea he was chief engineer on a 6000-ton supply ship — and one of the eleven survivors from 217 on board when a torpedo struck. Tom Pook earned his living from the sea for almost sixty years and in retirement in his seventies still takes a turn relieving on the Waiheke ferry.

For the family left at Puriri Point and the virtual second generation born after Tom's departure (Ted Pook was in his sixties when he fathered the 19th child — his 26th, counting both marriages) the traumatic manner of the oldest son's going somehow eased the pressure. Jolted in his tracks, Pook suffered a behavioural change, a mild one, but significant enough to spare the rest of the children Tom's ordeal. In any case, by the strength of her personality, Kohi had always provided them with support. Tall, large-boned, they had grown up around her a warm, close-knit family.

Life at the Point had its own problems. Getting to Arapaoa Native School on time was one of them. "Borer ate up our pendulum clock," Frank Pook recalls, "and the only other one in the house stopped if it was not kept face down. It was used only at baby feeding time." Leaving for school was regulated by the sound of the limeworks starting up over a mile away on the other shore. The noise of the machinery was also a compass in frequent heavy morning fog. Another navigational aid was a rope trailing behind the dinghy. Kohi lined it up with the coast and the children — never taking their eyes off it — had to row so that it remained at right angles to the stern. In rough weather school was not reached until late in the morning and if the weather deteriorated during the day they had to leave early.

At one period the school was run like a demented parade ground by an ex-British army sergeant-major. The commands and whistle blowing and marching and standing to attention carried right into the classroom where the national anthem was sung daily under the portrait of a uniformed George V. Not one word of Maori was permitted. In the playground some could not help themselves. Down came the rakau (stick) in a beating. The next teacher imposed almost as severe discipline, one observable difference being a leather cat-o-nine-tails to enforce the Maori embargo. At home Kohi Pook, fluent in Maori, deliberately spoke only English. Her visitors often laboured in broken English and the children secretly laughed at their mistakes. "Not until later," Bill Pook says, "did we realize that their struggle with conversation was to save us from being beaten at school." In bitter irony, the mother sometimes taught Pakeha children aspects of Maori culture. Her fascinating talks are still remembered.[8]

In household arrangements there were improvements. Vance Pook, the eighteenth born, recalls that a small reservoir was excavated at the spring below the cliff. It was close to high water and bulk supplies could be rowed back to the house in cream cans. "The water was lovely to drink but hard on the kettle — a thick limestone deposit meant it took hours to boil." One memorable year a shell concrete floor was put down in the chimney and a number 2 Dover stove installed. In winter the family sat in the chimney in a circle around its warmth — "It was an art to dodge the raindrops on a wet night" — and watched mangrove wood burn with a hot blue flame. The salt content of the wood caused two stoves to burn out in Vance's time.

And there were excitements from the outside world. Once a year Kuki Manukau, a hero of the Pahi regatta, arrived at Puriri Point. Unbeaten in the gruelling across-the-harbour horse race, he brought his champion with him to plough for the kumara crop. Since the horse swam around the harbour from one ploughing contract to another it was always in training for the great day.

The family itself, immaculately turned out, was part of the regatta. Mother

On Puriri Point with the youngest of the family — and only a few more to come.

always set up a stand to sell smoked mullet and father ran a ferry service between Pahi and Whakapirau. Bill Pook clearly remembers his first sight of Pahi on regatta day. It was not the boats and the bunting and the crowds that filled him with wonder but the distant sight of an enormous tree full of white leghorn hens. Why had they not left their roost at daybreak like the ones at home? When the family landed he learned that not all trees were puriris and karaka, particularly the domain's magnolia grandiflora in full blossom.

About once a year Ted Pook took the family on its own grand outing. They went down-harbour four miles to the south side of the Funnel entrance. Here they climbed to a high point on Hargreaves run. All the way a low prickly plant cruelly stabbed at their feet ("Dad had boots") but at the top they could see the Heads and a horizon running to infinity. And there was life out there apart from brother Tom. When Frank was fishing he dropped bottles with messages. One went from the Kaipara to the Manukau and drew a reply from Whatipu in less than a month. One dropped in 1939 was not found for more than forty years.

Seven of the Pook brothers became Kaipara fishermen and two of them were drowned at their work. When John tipped off his launch and was mutilated by the prop his body could not be found for some time. The area was made tapu. Ted Pook had shown little sympathy for Maori culture — the *Arizona's* original name, *Taranui*, had been scraped off because he thought it concerned female genitals[9] — but when Charlie Quaife, a Pakeha, set a net in the search area opposite the limeworks he readily agreed to the Maori search party using his launch for swift gunboat diplomacy. Quaife was run off the river.

Ted Pook showed signs of softening in old age. At the end of the war he built a better house at the Point for Kohi to rear the last 4 or 5 children. But he

Ted Pook hauls in another mountain of mullet. Young Tom and Bunnie Tilby at left.

was hard on himself to the last. He refused the pension until, with growing incapacity, Guy Jackman, the local storekeeper, persuaded him to make a claim. And although cancer of the jaw advanced until he was blinded, he refused to enter hospital. With fortitude that hardly bears contemplation, Kohi nursed her husband at the end as she had in the beginning. He died in 1948 at the age of 70.

Kohi stayed at the Point for five more years until her last son left school. To keep her hand in she cooked at the Pahi Hotel for a period and finally retired to live with daughter Marina in Auckland. She died in her 70th year in 1964.

Pook fishing boats — some of the best on the river — still ply out of Pahi and Whakapirau, at least one of them for frequent 7-day weeks. And for those of the family scattered far from the Kaipara the harbour is still a magnet. As this was being written, Mary, the first daughter born at Puriri Point, died with her husband in a car accident in Australia where she had lived for 25 years. Her body was brought back for burial in the family plot at Whakapirau in a cemetery above the water that daily washes her birthplace.

Vance (15), left, off to Wesley College in 1953, farewelled on Whakapirau wharf by Kohi and her youngest son, Clarence.

W. H. Stevens and Miss Pharoah about to enjoy another day of dalliance on the water.

7. Always a picnic at The Pines

We laze away the days or go fishing. — Ada Grace Pharoah.

"Would you care for a glass of wine?" Poised with sparkling decanter, wine of the best vintage, W.H. Stevens was always a gracious host. "I don't mind if I do," the rare local visitor might reply. "You don't mind?" Stevens would say, replacing the stopper and returning the decanter to its polished tray. "In that case we shan't bother."[1]

Stevens was not a man to tolerate what he considered to be a crassly colonial, ill-mannered response — or, for that matter, anything else he regarded as disturbing to his well-ordered existence. With one of the finest houses on the Kaipara, the richest furnishings, the most luxurious launch — all that and unlimited time and money to enjoy a life of unbroken idleness — why should he? Why, indeed.

The Stevens family were ironmongers, London-based, and rich. W.H. Stevens cashed in on the assets — by abusing a position of trust, some family members say, while his father was living in New Zealand for health reasons. (He died at Nelson in 1895.) Whatever, the oldest son, he ended up with the lion's share of the money.

William Henry Stevens came out to New Zealand with his wife Elizabeth and two sons, five and four years old, on the *China* in 1896. He came to retire on the Pahi River, a stone's throw across the water from where W.H. Colbeck had lived years before. Colbeck, that other William Henry, had come with single-minded devotion to the task of making more money; Stevens was equally

The Pines, side entrance, 1890s.

devoted to the enjoyment of what he already had.

Stevens had already visited New Zealand, to get the feel of the country and buy land. He had not rushed into retirement; the voyage of the *China* was merely the last stage of a slow boat to leisure. At 28 he was not pressed for time. The land chosen was on the Albertlander track that ran up to Paparoa from the head of the river. Its 230 acres sloped south-west to the water at the point where the Pahi Peninsula joined the steep hinterland, that region where, an early visitor had said, "Chaos and Creation must have had a hard fight of it just here."[2]

The house, named The Pines after a group of trees at the front gate, was sited well back from the water — it was hidden from the river except for distant glimpses — and tucked behind a bush-covered hill that gave concealment from the road. At some cost of winter sunshine it was utterly private.[3] Built to the design of an English country home, it was substantial, carefully detailed (even wooden brackets supporting the guttering were elegantly shaped) and immediately distinctive with small-paned casement windows instead of the customary double-hung of the period. Behind those little panes the place was stuffed with treasures.

All the furniture, the complete household contents, were shipped from England in zinc-lined cases and these were manhandled up the steep rise from the river. Every piece was superbly crafted, many already antiques of great value. The grandfather clock bore a mark where Lord Nelson had thrown a beer tankard, the massive wrought iron chandelier had been fabricated by an expert employed to work on fittings in St Pauls Cathedral. And with their iron trade connections the family had been able to commission more works from this craftsman. Stevens brought out tall firedogs with spitting dragon faces[4]

98

The Pines, seaward side, and Miss Pharoah's cottage.

and delicate, tendril-twining lamp standards — another side to the supply of cast iron manhole covers on London's sewers that still bear the firm's name.

The walls of The Pines were hung with sober portraits, heirloom tapestries and lithographs of grand events — all in gilded frames — and throughout the house, china cabinets, chiffoniers, oak shelves and table tops were stacked with silverware, crystal, fine china and pewter. One kitchen dresser displayed a museum list of early English copper vessels — sturdy kettles, billies, flour sifters and sieves, long handled dippers, fat Guernsey Island milk jugs. Even an ashtray was a model of the coppersmith's art, the medallion set in lead in its base a 1796 tuppenny piece, newly minted. In every room, on every surface, opulence and abundance.

There was a butler. Frank Stevens, W.H. Steven's younger brother, a bachelor, lived permanently at The Pines and served as the butler. He also tended the strictly formal English garden at the approach to the house where roses were confined according to variety within a series of tightly trimmed box-hedge enclosures.

As with the art regimented along the walls inside where no colour splashed or wayward brush strokes were permitted, there was no place in the gardener's art for the intrusion of spontaneity. The only free forms to be found at The Pines were those climbing lamp standard tendrils everlastingly captured in wrought iron. And guarding them, on closer look, could be seen the faces of demons.

Stevens supervised his rose garden, he studied lower life through a powerful microscope, he played the piano and he fished. His pursuits and his hobbies did not rob him of the time to enforce his wishes in household matters. The boys (but not the parents) were required to take a cold bath every day and, like the

W. H. Stevens — two studies of the "Commander".

observance of sit-up-straight no-cushions-allowed rules, this was closely monitored. Still remembered in the district — with different degrees of fascination depending on personal ideology — was the Stevens instruction that the large fireplaces be supplied with a precise number of logs. He counted the firewood and sent it back if there was one log too many or one too few. Not for nothing did Elizabeth Stevens, a small, gentle woman, the daughter of a clergyman, always refer to her husband as "the Commander."

The dinner table was a place where authority could not be escaped. A daughter-in-law, about to enter her 90th year when interviewed, still sharply remembers the peremptory tone from the head of the table. "Pepper? Yes or No!" A niece who was allergic to milk as a child recalls being forced to empty her glass no matter that her stomach quickly followed suit. Miss Pharoah, the hostess (of whom more later) was an expert cook who presented the meal beautifully. Her recollection of her aunt is of a quiet woman who sat at the far end of the table where the food was not so abundant and where stale bread was stacked.

Stevens encouraged other members of his family to migrate to New Zealand. Brothers Sydney and Percy came to farm at Paparoa and sister Alice, product of an exclusive school and "delicate" — she was much given to tonic wine — lived for a time at The Pines before marrying the Pahi schoolteacher-turned-farmer, Tom Skelton. Another sister stayed briefly, didn't warm to the place, and returned to England.

Percy, not as adaptable to farm life as Sydney, became the district photographer. He married Mary Adams, the Hukatere orchardist's daughter, and later opened his own studio in Karangahape Road, Auckland. In all the hundreds of photographs he took, always signed and dated, there is not one of that most photogenic of places, The Pines. For one reason or another — and marriage against his wishes to locals was in the forefront — Stevens broke off connections with his two brothers. His sister's marriage to a Skelton passed — they were Anglo-Irish gentry from County Fermagh — and Frank, of course, remained in favour.

Stevens lived a world away from his neighbours. From the day he arrived to the day he died he took the English society journals, the *Tatler*, the *Sketch* and the *Bystander* — all still carefully stacked in the zinc-lined cases that brought the furniture. The regular columns, Our Riviera Letter, The Highway of Fashion, and the regular social rounds, the hunt and hunt balls, country house parties, the coming out of titled debutantes, a dowager's soiree — all preserved, for this was about regular people, the sort who knew how to accept wine graciously.

Jane Mander's *The Story of a New Zealand River* has one of her characters, Mrs Blayton (Mrs Susannah Clayton of Kaiwaka), saying ". . .Auckland. They call it a city, that little village! I don't care if I never see it again. No. Give me my garden and my view of the river, and the smell of burnt fern and my English papers." To attend to his investments Stevens did visit Auckland, staying at the best private hotels, and there would have been little pungency from a burn-off on his property since only enough was cleared for house cows, but the novel's sense of voluntary exile, smug and self-sufficient, is accurate for him. Through his English papers Stevens remained vicariously in touch with "the best people" and, apart from a small matter of 12,000 miles, he stayed one of them.

So much more devastating then, when Elizabeth bore him a child who was less than perfect. His daughter Violet was born crippled, incurably so, and was carried on a litter and later, before she died in her sixth or seventh year, moved about in a donkey cart. Stevens laid the blame on his wife and, it is said, barely spoke to her again.

The Stevens boys and their butler uncle.   Percy Stevens, photographer.

Ada Grace Pharoah — two studies of a "governess".

The two sons, William Henry (the fourth generation of eldest sons to carry that name) and Norman, were not permitted to attend school. Miss Pharoah, an old friend of Stevens from England, who came at the turn of the century on a recuperative visit after an unhappy love affair, stayed on to live permanently at The Pines. She gave them tuition. Miss Pharoah, now 27, had moved freely in London society; one suitor, it is said, was an admiral who had drowned, another was the young Mr Rolls, son of Lord Llangattock, who imported the third motor car into Britain and gave his name to a partnership with a Mr Royce. (He died in 1910 at the age of 33 in a fall from an aeroplane.)

Miss Pharoah, well-educated, musical, and variously talented, had a cottage

The interior of Miss Pharoah's cottage. The fourth wall has french doors to a verandah.

provided for her a few paces from the side door to The Pines. It was built as one large room with a fireplace, a verandah running its full length and a bay window view of the river. A bed was tucked into a sunny corner. As lavishly furnished as the house, but decorated in wallpaper with fashionable broad vertical stripes and hung with pictures displaying a more sophisticated taste, the room was more inviting and offered altogether brighter prospects of relaxation than its heavily formal neighbour.

Another luxuriously appointed adjunct to The Pines was *Nautilus*, a 30-foot pleasure launch built in 1907. It was equipped to a standard almost unknown at that time. Stevens had ordered a launch from the prestigious Auckland shipbuilders, Bailey and Lowe, took a trial run on the Waitemata, and sent it back. Their second try was accepted.[5] The *Nautilus* was not quite as long, but whether this was the reason for rejecting the first boat is unknown. Perhaps it was simply the log of firewood routine writ somewhat larger.

The *Nautilus* was delivered by sailing round North Cape and Thomas Downes, a master woodworker who had come to the Kaipara to escape the bottle, was engaged to complete the furnishings. Downes had been employed on finishing work at The Pines — carved black manuka bases on the wrought iron lamp standards were examples of his versatility and skill. The *Nautilus*, too, had special light fittings in the sumptuous sleeping quarters, a library, and a stove to cook fish straight from the sea. Heavy with three skins of kauri, she was built for comfort and safety, not speed.

Stevens responded to the splendour of his craft by adding a nautical cap to his standard formal attire. He had whiled away 10 years in a Kaipara punt and a small launch with a simple dodger, now he could cruise and explore far reaches of the harbour. As Miss Pharoah wrote on the back of a photograph of an idyllic stretch of water, "We laze away the days or go fishing." Not a governess, but rather a member of the household, she did not satisfy the boys' educational ambitions. Forbidden to further their schooling in the outside world they sometimes slipped away in the evenings to visit the home of E.W. Stephenson, the Paparoa headmaster, and took secret lessons from him.

Such rebellion could only end in conflict with the Commander. And grievous conflict came when they were young adults, the issue, marriage. Stevens considered no New Zealand woman to be a fit companion for a son of his. They were better unmarried than pulled down to that level. He wanted

Elegant stairs to an attic bedroom at The Pines.

them to find suitable brides in England. If they defied him he promised to cut them off from their inheritance. They did and they were.

In their mid-twenties, first Billy and then Norman married young women (cousins) from the old-established Massey family of Maungaturoto. For Billy, life was difficult, he was briefly married three times and died at 45 of a brain tumour. Norman, who married in 1917, became a successful farmer by his own efforts and the husband and father of a loving family.

Kitchen dresser loaded with a dozen fine jugs and other quality china.

A corner of the billiard room.

Meanwhile their place was taken by an 18-year-old youth who arrived from England. Treated as a son by both Miss Pharoah and W.H. Stevens, the young Englishman lived permanently at The Pines. He was joined later by a young friend who had travelled to New Zealand on the same ship. Mrs Stevens, a devoted Christian, adapted with fortitude to the arrangements made around her.

With his unsuitably married sons suitably banished — and replaced — another shadow, however, lay on Steven's long, lazy horizon. Preoccupation with the preservation of a sound social order was second to concern for the soundness of his own body. There had been intimations of morbid concern when he reacted so violently to the birth of a handicapped daughter; as the years idled by those worries intensified. He suffered migraine attacks and other ill-defined maladies. He developed a close relationship with Dr Dukes, a local medical practitioner well known for his idiosyncratic ways. On a bad morning the Commander would come in to breakfast feeling his pulse and threatening to sell up the home. "I'm off to the Islands with Dukie," was one of his heartrending cries.

Two young men coming or two going — whichever, Miss Pharoah presides at the gate.

The search for health took him on more frequent visits to Auckland. Accompanied by Miss Pharoah, he stayed for days at a time, finding particular relief at the hands (literally) of Mrs Pilgrim, a well-known Khyber Pass healer. The wife of a flourmill owner, six-foot tall, red-headed Ada Pilgrim was a woman of great presence who used her gift for people and not for money. She was a daughter of John Chadwick and — small world department — had spent her early years at Pahi. Stevens presented her with some fine pieces of china and they are still in the possession of the Chadwick family.[6]

Not surprisingly it was Elizabeth Stevens, prematurely aged, whose health seriously failed. In her last years her son and daughter-in-law took her away from The Pines and nursed her until she died. On the Kaipara she left no trace. In all the albums of photographs of The Pines, its people and their possessions not one has been found of Mrs Stevens — perhaps none was ever taken. The only relic is a letter of condolence Stevens received on her death — and that was given to a neighbour for its amusement value. It reads:

> Mr Willie Stevens
>   Dear Mr Stevens
> We didn't hear of your wifes deth till now or some of us would of been to the funereale. How many children have you if you have remember them to me Gordon tell me you have to in one house where he took the fish round thank you for the money you give Ella hoping you are well as I have a bad cold God be with you till we meat again
>   — Mrs Carl Gulbransen[7]

Defective spelling massaged his sense of superiority as did artless curiosity about his domestic arrangements. But Stevens's turn came.

Among the stacks of society journals stored today in a farm shed at The Pines is a pile of *Physical Culture* magazines. They date from the Commander's last years and carry such messages as "Build Body Vigor — Sleep on a Hard Bed" and "Habits That Kill — Are You Heading for an Early Grave Because of Your Pet Indulgences?" One headline reads: Bernard Macfadden in his Personal Message This Month Discusses — PROLONGING YOUR LIFE. But the body of W.H. Stevens had already decided for itself that thirty years of self-indulgence was long enough. As he reached sixty, Steven's health deteriorated. For one thing he could not sleep. He had the young English arrival sit beside the bed gripping his hand throughout the night and his presence brought some relief. On 22 April 1927, at the age of 63, he died of a stroke. Two years later, Frank Stevens, the faithful butler, died at 62 from a coronary. Over the strenuous opposition of Miss Pharoah, some of his money was bequeathed to his nephews.

After the death of W.H.Stevens, Ada Grace Pharoah was mistress of The Pines for nine years — apart from a return visit to England accompanied by the young Englishman. She too died at a comparatively early age — at 62 in 1936 — after a long, trying illness. She had hyperpiesia, defined as "an abnormally high blood pressure occurring independently of any discoverable organic disease."

The land and the house and its furnishings were all left to the young man who arrived from England. One exception was the four Stevens family heirlooms, the framed tapestries, "magnificent examples of 19th century needlework", which Miss Pharoah bequeathed to the Auckland Museum.[8] Some cash and her motorcar went to the second young man. The legitimate sons, as instructed by the Commander, inherited nothing.

Ellen Blackwell on a visit to The Pines. With two exceptions (pp. 113, 123) all photographs in this chapter are by Frank Blackwell, most of them developed from glass negatives.

8. The silencing of Frank Blackwell's sister

Love-tokens are said to have been made by the Maoris . . . from strips of flax leaves. A double slip knot was formed, which, if tightly pulled, ran into one large single knot. The double loop was presented by the young Maori to his sweetheart, who signified her consent to his silent proposal by drawing the two knots into one.

— Laing and Blackwell, *Plants of New Zealand*, 1906

Since purchasing my first copy of *Plants of New Zealand* as a schoolboy the name Blackwell has been something of a mystery to me . . . The usual sources of biographical information about botanists . . . provided nothing.

— Dr A. Thomson, *Botany Division Newsletter*,
DSIR, December, 1985.

Ellen Blackwell's voyage to New Zealand on the passenger liner *Omrah* began ordinarily enough. Forty-two, unmarried, deeply interested in botany and the author of religious books for children, she was part of that heavy traffic where the comfortable Edwardian-English middle class checked out on migrating relatives, sampled the colonial life, and reported back home with a bundle of Rotorua postcards.

Ellen's brothers Frank and William had been in New Zealand for 24 years. They had returned for a visit but it was a long time ago. Their partnership on the Pahi River had ended with William's marriage. He was in Auckland. Frank, amateur botanist, talented photographer, and now married himself, still lived the back-to-the-land life of a fugitive from industrial Britain. His early accounts of ominous rumblings heard at Pahi when Tarawera erupted had quietened to somewhat less alarming descriptions of the Kaipara's daily round. But his zany rhyming letters and loving camera studies continued to fire the imagination back home. Earnest, faintly forbidding in steel spectacles, and supported by a school teacher niece as travelling companion, Ellen was tilted towards adventure.

By 1903 the voyage out offered easy progress through the Suez with plenty of exotic calls. At Naples a New Zealander boarded the *Omrah*. His name was Robert Laing and he proved to be a schoolmaster, a bachelor her own age — and a botanist. They joined forces for trips ashore and on reaching New Zealand the foundation of one of the country's most successful literary collaborations had been cemented.

But first Ellen visited Frank at Pahi. After the train and the steamer there was a bumpy ride by buggy along the spine of the peninsula and down through an

Green-clad Karepo and KKK, the children's cottage. Note young oak (obscured, right, with shadow), today an outstanding tree.

avenue of wattles to a vine-clad house by the sea. A rambling, comfortable, unpretentious and thoroughly welcoming house. No cleverly turned verandah posts, no mail order fretwork, no decorated bargeboards — four finials the only concession to Victorian ornamentation. It was called Karepo (a salt water grass) after the surrounding block of land.

The house had grown from a gabled rectangle set lengthwise to the water. This had been doubled in size with a second, parallel gable, and then two wings had been added at right angles to give a sheltered central verandah looking across mangroves to the river.   For the children a standard attic-bedroomed colonial cottage had been barged in and sited on a rise some distance away. Like everything else Frank Blackwell designed, his housing arrangements were original, sensible — and a shade more expensive that the average settler could afford.

Apprenticed to an ironmonger at fifteen, Frank was told after contracting rheumatic fever that he would not survive the English climate. In 1881 at the age of nineteen, he left for New Zealand. Brother William, two years older, went with him. Their father had done well in the drapery trade and owned eighteen houses in the Midlands city of Northampton. A leading Baptist with Albertlander contacts, he steered his sons towards the Kaipara and in 1883 financed the purchase of the 82-acre Karepo block on the left bank of the Pahi River just before Tokatapu. The land cost £250 and Frank later bought out his brother's share for £150.[1]

Frank Blackwell aimed at self-sufficiency. He kept bees, milked a housecow, raised ducks and hens and planted a half-acre orchard. The grazing land was leased to nearby farmer George New and rather than clear the bush on the

Queuing for repairs at Blackwell's wharf.

property he reclaimed tidal flats to grow maize for poultry and oats for the horses. He built a boathouse, used it as a workshop to make his own Kaipara punt, and constructed an impressive wharf over an eighth of a mile long. He turned his hand to everything from gumdigging and cocksfoot harvesting to launch maintenance. The district still remembers him as "a clever engineer" who made major repairs to one launch engine by dovetailing together the broken parts of a flywheel cog, a job that normally would have had to go away for expensive welding.[2] Some might marvel at a self-sufficiency that included turning his own tea tree knitting needles on a lathe — for knitting his own socks.

A dashing apiarist in boater and boots, Frank Blackwell charms a swarm of bees.

A source of cash income was photography and, to a minor extent, picture framing. Blackwell spent days in the darkroom producing postcards. For one who had embraced, along with the anti-mass production philosophy of the arts and crafts movement, the exaggerated British passion for the rural picturesque (two reactions to urban ugliness and industrial squalor), it was appropriate that he should label several sets of postcards "Picturesque Pahi", "Picturesque Pahi River" and "Picturesque Paparoa".

If he shared a third strand of 19th century longing — the romantic vision of South Seas indolence providing sub-tropical plenty — the Kaipara, for all its balmy days, was the place to get jolted into reality. In the spring of 1890 his diary thankfully records the end to days of heavy labour cutting tea tree. But rejoicing was premature:

> Monday, Sept 29. Mr Upton came up for stakes. He and I loaded it, [the punt], with 900. Started down at 11, anchored off his point till 11 at night, then went up the creek. Unloaded while standing in water, back to the house at 1.30 completely done up. Slept on the sofa. Showery. Tuesday, Sept. 30. Had very little sleep for mosquitoes, up at 5 baling out punt. Started up creek at 9, loaded and started back at 10.30. Got well out into the creek when it began to blow a stiff breeze or more right ahead. Had to anchor and wait, shivering one and a half hours in pouring, driving rain and sleet, waiting for wind to drop. Gave it up then went back to the house and waited for right tide. Just starting when visitors turned up . . . Finished unloading 1.30. Home at 3am cold and wet.[3]

In 1898 Frank Blackwell's father died leaving him £6000, a considerable sum. It did not change his enjoyment of the simple life. As he wrote to a daughter years later, "The Uptons are coming tonight to hear the Rev. Lionel Fletcher discourse on 'The Greatest Danger in New Zealand.' Dancing, I suppose, or smoking or drinking or racing or gambling. Goodness! did it ever strike you what an angelic father you have who doesn't do any of these things."

Nor did money change his attitude to society. It is expressed in these verses, the first and last of a poem mocking the use of "Esquire" behind the name of some of his neighbours.

E.S.Q.

I wonder what these letters mean,
I wonder if they show,
That some are stationed high in life
And some are stationed low!
If yea, I wonder which they mark,
I cannot tell — can you
Whether 'tis credit or a shame
To be an E.S.Q.

I'm no reformer; would not choose
To make myself a mark
For custom's arrows, while her curs
In stupid chorus bark.
Follow the fashion, if you please,
It may be meet for you,
But let me shoot for rarer game
Than common E.S.Q.[4]

Land reclaimed from the tide. Today the tide has reclaimed its own.

Frank and Nan Blackwell on their
wedding day, 21-2-1900.

His diary now recorded more botanical observations, the house was
enlarged, and in 1900 at the age of 38 he married Nan (Annie) Browne (31),
daughter of an Auckland accountant and sister of the Pahi postmistress, Mrs
Matilda Cuttle. Nan had broken off an engagement because of her fiance's
alcoholism and Blackwell, among his other assets, was a teetotaller.

When his sister Ellen Blackwell and her niece Annie arrived in January 1904,
two of the couple's three children had been born. Life had become leisurely
enough for Annie to recall (in an exercise book when in her eighties) that "Here
we spent the summer and enjoyed many happy outings — picnics being a
favourite means of bringing the scattered settlers together to enjoy fishing,
swimming and boating on the Pahi River."[5]

Annie became engaged to Heber Skelton of Paparoa and after returning to
England for several years to complete a contract to teach deaf children, she
came back to marry him. For Ellen it was a summer stay that extended over
three more summers. Entranced by the New Zealand bush she set out in
collaboration with her shipboard friend, Robert Laing, to produce a book that
would fire the public with her enthusiasm. It was secular evangelism at its best
and she enlisted her brother Frank to travel the country with her photographing
and researching.

Published in 1906, *Plants of New Zealand* by Laing and Blackwell, "with 160
Original Photographs by E.W. and F.B. Blackwell," was a remarkable work. It
was unique for the number and quality of illustrations — and the single largest
source of these was Pahi. It was also unique in its wide-ranging approach. Far
more than a botany text, it interwove aspects of Pakeha and Maori life into its
scientific framework.

High tide among the mangroves.

For the bulk of the population botany badly needed popularising. As Dr. Leonard Cockayne said in a review of the book (he was himself preparing a popular work), New Zealand was an agricultural country "and yet to nearly everybody this science is a dead letter. There are thousands indeed, who do not know the name of a single plant, let alone its habits." Ellen Blackwell's Kaipara references are good examples of how the book set out to reach such readers. It is not difficult to place the source of this cabbage tree anecdote (a creek ran to the tide on Blackwell's farm):

> These plants are wonderfully tenacious of life — indeed it seems to be almost impossible to kill them. A number of trees were once cut down and thrown over a fence on to the shingly beach of a creek. For eight months they lay there, rolling up and down in the salt tide, or baking high and dry in the sun. At last an exceptionally high tide lifted them back again over the fence into the paddock. As soon as they found themselves upon soil once more, they sent out rootlets, and shortly afterwards were seen to be budding vigorously.

A second example of their hardiness was a Northland gumdigger's chimney made by nailing together cabbage tree trunks set in a trench. After burning a continuous fire for months he left and the "blackened chimney became a mass of living green."

114

Protective fencing for a six-headed nikau.

In the same popular vein the Kaipara provided a freak, six-headed nikau (photographed) and oysters gathered on pohutukawa branches "almost dipping into the sea" give a strong image of the Christmas tree coastline along parts of old Pahi. More soberly, a three page unravelling of the puzzling metamorphosis of the lancewood from spiky-stiff, leather-leafed juvenile to gracious tree was demonstrated by specimens gathered around the Kaipara in eight distinct stages of development.

Early botanists had put mature and immature forms of the same plant in different genera. "Even so late as 1867 Sir J. Hooker, one of the greatest of all systemists," had been confused, she wrote, "and yet he had had the plant under cultivation at Kew for fifteen years!"

Closer to home the riddle had been solved but the book could still tilt at nodding authority. A statement on the lancewood by Thomas Kirk in his *Forest Flora*, it said, "scarcely seems to be accurate . . . in the Kaipara district at least."

The Kaipara influence is strongest in Ellen Blackwell's section on the mangrove. For the kauri, "one of the most magnificent timber trees known," she gave more space than any other forest tree — seven pages. For the lowly mangrove it was ten pages. They included three full page plates — one of the flower, one of the fruit, one of the twisted trunks — and a half-page picture, complete with Frank Blackwell in punt, of Pahi mud flats pushing up aerial roots. A half-century ahead of her time Ellen Blackwell saw beauty in the mangrove and deftly answered its detractors. She quoted, "from one of the earliest New Zealand novels,"[6] this "impassioned but somewhat inaccurate description":

> Oh! those mangroves. I never saw one that looked as if it possessed a decent conscience. Growing always in shallow stagnant water, filthy black mud, or rank grass, gnarled, twisted, stunted and half-bare of foliage, they seem like crowds of withered, trodden down old criminals,condemned to the punishment of everlasting life. I can't help it if this seems fanciful. Anyone who has seen a mangrove swamp will know what I mean.

The mangrove's "evil reputation" partly arose from the prevalence of malaria in tropical river estuaries, Ellen Blackwell explained. "Miasmatic vapours were supposed to arise from the pestilential mangrove swamps, and spread their contagion around. Science had not then burdened the misguided mosquito with sins of transmission, as well as of commission.

Frank Blackwell delighted in gliding his punt through silent mangrove channels, and his children staked out their own private trees to perch in. His daughter, Florence (Billie) Guinness, recalls that they gave each tree a name — she cannot remember her own but the biggest, claimed by older brother, Frank Jr, was "the Grand Hotel." (Once he fell out of the Grand Hotel while reading and surfaced from the bottom of the channel still clutching *The Boys Own.*)

Such pleasures would have seemed cranky indeed in 1906. Ellen Blackwell contented herself with writing that "at high tide, a mangrove swamp is often a pleasant place to punt in, for then the somewhat sickly odour of the mud is replaced by the fresh smell of the sea."

The Blackwells made a massive contribution to *Plants in New Zealand*. Ellen's hand was present in both the descriptive and scientific text through the book and she was entirely responsible for three main sections.[7] They were the pine family — kauri, totara, rimu, kahikatea, matai, miro; the palm family — five photographic studies of the nikau; and the lily family — most prominently supplejack, cabbage tree and flax. In addition to supplying photographs and his own botanical observations, Frank assisted Ellen in preparing the index to its 456 pages.

Robert Laing had a science degree and an intimate knowledge of the South Island and his strengths dominated. But while it was not strictly scientific of his co-author to attribute murderous intentions to the rata vine — Ellen's caption to one of her brother's photographs read, "Rata *(Metrosideros robusta)* attempting to strangle Puriri *(Viten lucens)*" and the text referred to the puriri as "apparently the only tree which can resist this iron hug" — it was such fanciful flights that endeared this book, and the bush, to generations of New Zealanders.

But Ellen Blackwell was a woman, and a visiting one who dared correct publicly the errors of old guard male botanists — Sir Joseph Hooker, as we have seen, and typically Thomas Kirk, whose *Forest Flora*, among numerous glaring mistakes on the mangrove, thought its aerial roots were growing stems.

There was a nudge, wink to reviews. It was an "open secret", they said, that

Ellen Blackwell is entertained at The Pines by Miss Pharoah, right.

the book was Laing's work. The suggestion hung in the air that a romantic attachment to the English visitor had led him to make a gift of unearned authorship. One of the most blatant offenders was Dr Leonard Cockayne who spoke of Laing's "brilliant word-painting" and declared the "open secret" to be justification for using his name only throughout a lengthy review in the Christchurch *Press*.[8] And Laing, a teacher at Christchurch Boys' High School, failed to put the record straight. A shy, diffident man, it was not for nothing that the boys had soon changed his nickname "Dog" — earned by a fierce bulldog expression — to "Puppy Laing."

The campaign was ugly enough to prompt an Auckland clergyman, the Rev. T.F. Robertson, to write a 1000-word article for the *New Zealand Herald* in Ellen Blackwell's defence.[9] It was headlined "Miss E.W. Blackwell — Her Services to the Literature of New Zealand." Quoting Cockayne without naming him, Robertson spoke of her modesty preventing a lawsuit. He fantasised "the fearful thought" of giving the critic "a public scourging" — with a bush-lawyer! — and settled for "a Christian and chivalrous duty to repudiate . . . unjust and unkind treatment of a lady. . ."

Robertson reversed Cockayne's order of things. "Miss Blackwell felt, as many

Nan Blackwell pours, Frank nurses the baby, niece Annie from England at left.

before her, the need of some trustworthy guide to the treasures of nature of a more popular order than the standard writings of Cheeseman, Kirk and Hooper. . ." It was her "expenditure of much toil, strength and money" and her "gentle and unselfish influence" that had inspired Laing to join in.

And Frank Blackwell, also ignored, was given his due. She had been able to write "in the pleasant rural home of a brother, in sympathy with her efforts, and whose careful observation of nature and artistic tastes have been of great service in the work. . ."

Robertson neatly turned Cockayne's attack. Her description of the breathing roots of mangroves was "ascribed by a leading scientific critic in Christchurch . . . to the brilliant pen of Mr Laing — the highest possible compliment surely to the scientific and literary ability of Miss Blackwell."

The article dismayed Ellen Blackwell. She had not helped in the preparation of her defense, indeed, knew nothing about it. Robertson, a friend of her brother, had written on his own initiative. She wrote to the *Herald* and to Cockayne, Laing and the botanist Thomas Cheeseman, distancing herself from the fray.

Cheeseman had helped her to identify specimens for the book, including some she had gathered in an expedition to Ball Hut on Mt Cook. Climbing over male bastions was clearly not part of her purpose:

> I should like to take the opportunity of clearing myself in your eyes as regards the article. . . You will have naturally thought like everyone else that it had my consent and approval. It had neither and nothing could have annoyed me more. . . I believe that he thought he was doing me a kindness and does not seem to understand the wrongful and unpleasant position in which he has placed me.[10]

Her discretion is understandable. If not wrongful it would have been certainly unpleasant to tangle with Cockayne. For all his distinction he held views on the human female as crudely unscientific as the rest of society. When Amy Castle, entomologist at the Dominion Museum, attempted to ask him a question on cross-breeding in native flora at a meeting of the Wellington Philosophical Society he refused to answer. Sexual matters, he said, could not be discussed with a lady. [11] And that was twenty-five years after Ellen Blackwell had dared trespass into his territory!

Ellen Blackwell returned to England after her book came out, later married, and never revisited this country. *Plants of New Zealand* went on to become a New Zealand classic. It was in demand for over sixty years and ran to seven editions.* By 1962, when over 23,000 copies had been sold with the last edition still to come, its brilliant success was recognized by the journal of the Royal New Zealand Horticultural Society in an article, "Robert Malcolm Laing, 1865-1941."[12] Laing had published many papers, it said, (one with Cockayne in 1911), but the "real foundation" of his reputation was *Plants of New Zealand*. Dr H.H. Allan, Director of the DSIR Botany Division, was quoted; "Many generations will yet draw inspiration from the pages of this classic work."

But Ellen Blackwell? ". . .it has been what is known as an open secret that the book is almost entirely the work of R.M. Laing. Miss Ellen Blackwell. . . seems to be something of a mystery."

All those years and still the same "open secret." She "helped with some of the classifications and supplied 160 photographs . . . while her brother F.B. Blackwell helped with indexing." And a new twist: "There is a tale of romance between the two authors. Miss Blackwell went home to England and Laing went haring after her, had no luck and returned home to remain a bachelor to the end of his days. There is no truth in this little bit of gossip and I mention it only to kill it. Laing did go for a trip to England, but it was in 1903 and the *Plants of New Zealand* didn't see the light of day until 1906."

Not gossip killed, just gossip wounded with half-truths. Ellen Blackwell was spared the nonsense. She died at Portsmouth in her 88th year in 1952.[13]

Meanwhile Frank Blackwell, whose photographic credits were dropped from later editions, had made a reputation as an author in his own right. He became a leading contributor to the Rationalist magazine, the *Truthseeker*. His background was strongly religious: his father a prominent Baptist, his mother the grand-daughter of a Baptist clergyman, two of his sisters missionaries in India (one dying there) and the third, Ellen, author of a bulky life of Jesus and other religious books for children. The 1976 jubilee booklet of St Marks, Paparoa, lists him as an Anglican and his wife (not listed) worked hard for the

---

* Cockayne's *N.Z. Plants and Their Story*, published 1910, went out of print after the third edition, 1927.

Last of the giants? A district send-off for a big one on the bush tramway.

church and taught Sunday School at their house.

But Blackwell broke with all that. Perhaps he was influenced as a young man by neighbour Henry Scotland's unorthodox religious views. And the brother of Heber Skelton who had married his niece, the lawyer Alfred Hall Skelton, had become a leading Rationalist.[14] But certainly with his voracious reading and "loner" temperament he would have had no difficulty in reaching his own conclusions.

The precept and example of his devout father were a likely catalyst. A relative had been slow to repay a loan to Frank Blackwell and his father declared that he, too, had been "awfully imposed upon." He wrote from England to New Zealand:

> Do not trust in a man or a woman, a parson or a priest, nor brother nor sister . . . this is the best advice I can give you. Read this carefully and prayerfully and the Lord guide and bless you in all things.
>
> Your affectionate father,
John Blackwell.[15]

The father died in 1898, disinheriting his crippled eldest son who had worked hard but unsuccessfully at the family business. The beneficiaries, Frank and

A superb study of Norwegian neighbours, the Gulbransens.

William in New Zealand and Arthur, an English surgeon, clubbed together to give their brother his share.

Corresponding years later with a former Pahi farm worker, Clive Kingsley-Smith, Frank Blackwell wrote:

I have become the last few years in spite of early training, long associations, and even wishes, an anti-orthodox Xtian. I simply cannot 'believe' as I used to do, or more accurately, used to think I did for I am convinced that very few indeed could now really believe the various things required in the creeds etc. if they studied the evidence available. . . I've studied religion from every point of view I could get and came to the conclusion that the Golden Rule is the safest form and just about all that's necessary.

So many Gods, so many creeds,
So many paths that wind & wind,
While just the art of being kind
Is all this old world needs.

I'm not sure whose that is, or if it's word correct, but it's good enough for me.[16]

Frank Blackwell died at the age of 72 in 1934. His life after death is an enviable one. Pahi resident Stella Fenwick has memories of moonlight picnics he organized up the river when she was a young woman but, above all, she remembers the special quality of childhood visits to the Blackwell's before the first world war.

About to launch into space on the "Giant Stride".

"There was a kind of maypole we whirled around on, and swings and a three-storey dolls house with stairs. There were all kinds of unusual things. He cut a hole in the oven door and put in a window — the first we'd ever heard of that idea. And he made a kitchen step-ladder that folded on hinges to make a chair." Blackwell was small, slightly built, self-effacing, and a trace self-conscious about his premature baldness. "He stayed in the background but you knew he was a precise man — even a bit fussy."

His daughter, Billie Guinness, says "the maypole" was in fact "the giant stride," a pole with a ring at the top turning on ball bearings. Ropes hung from the ring. "The faster you ran, the higher you got — we went sky high."

Her father, a vigorous tennis player until 70, (he made the concrete roller for the Pahi grass court) also believed in exercise for the children and there was a horizontal bar as well as swings. And he made water sleds for aqua-planing on the river. "We practically lived at the river — either in it or on it. As small children we would just drift with the tide spearing flounder from the boat. We were treated as equals — I had one of the first driving licenses in the district* — and as a girl I was encouraged to saw wood, hammer or paint. He was always making something and he was a perfectionist."

Billie Guinness has handsome kauri cabinets, a box inlaid with over a hundred pieces of native timber, and hand-made kaleidoscopes. "Father tapered coloured glass into triangles and made dozens of kaleidoscopes for fund-raising at local bazaars. He also gave them to Auckland orphanages. That was typical, of course. During the big flu epidemic he stripped the citrus trees and sent all the fruit to Auckland Hospital."

The generosity of the Blackwells is recalled by Gladys Stevens (nee Massey) of Pukekohe. "KKK, Karepo Kamp Kottage, the second house, was always

* Issued 1925 after Billie (19) had been driving for a year. The county clerk said there was no need for a test — he had been watching her.

overflowing with young people at holiday time. There was no funnier place —
something amusing was always going on. At the table, if you wanted food
passed, you had to make your request rhyme with the last word of the
previous speaker — and no butter or sugar if you forgot. Frank Blackwell was
bursting with humour but he never smiled and that made it all the funnier."

Gladys Stevens grew up to be a tree-lover and approaching her 90th year she
has clear memories of the Blackwell's bush. Preserving and planting native trees
— that was a serious subject. And Billie Guinness recalls that every Sunday
afternoon her father took the family for bush walks, pointing out natural
wonders, naming trees. And trees are Frank Blackwell's monument.

Great trees now frame the site where the house once stood. A row of
Californian redwoods front the water and behind them stand two rare pecan
nut trees, particularly fine specimens. Behind them again on this sheltering ridge
to the north of the site is an Australian silky oak and a Japanese camphor tree.

The young English oak beside the house that gave shade to babies sleeping in
a hanging cradle beside the house has grown to a magnificent giant that dwarfs
the observer. And where the house garden once flourished is a grove of big-
stemmed bamboo and a tangle of shrubs and vines — red-flowered mallow,
oleander, wild or cultivated olive, false acacia, escallonia, and the Chinese
trumpet vine.

In the patch of original bush that gives shelter from the south, wistaria
scrambles through puriri and rimu and other natives and at its edge two
cabbage trees support enormous collars of staghorn. They are over 20 feet (6m)
in circumference.

On high ground behind the site the bare trunk of an exotic palm rises from
a clump of date palms and soars to a 70-foot (21m) fan-topped silhouette on the
skyline. It is a distant marker from Pahi Road and from out to sea for what
was once, in the botanist Dr Robert Cooper's measured words, "clearly a
garden of character and quality."

Of all the forgotten gardens that ring the Kaipara, Blackwell's is the most
impressive. It deserves to become a place of pilgrimage.

HON. H. SCOTLAND, M.L.C.

One man bars the way to the Transvaal contingent, *Christchurch Press* cartoon, 1899.

9. A party of one

No doubt it is exceedingly convenient for the upper classes, who are living upon the accumulated abuses of many centuries, that certain things should not be called by their proper names. Of one thing, however, I am quite certain: pretty speaking never won us our liberties, and courtly phrases will not preserve them for us.

— Henry Scotland, *The New Zealander on London Bridge*, 1878

Near the centre of the wide curve of Aute Bay, midway up Pahi River, two magnolias bloom each summer. They grow at the edge of the land where a clay bank drops to the shelly beach. Approached from the sea, bare paddocks rise behind to the ridge of the peninsula where the Pahi road runs, but on the flat ground around the magnolias a clump of eleagnus sprawls and thickets of ivy and rambler rose send climbing shoots up cabbage trees. In this remnant of an old garden a gatepost leans, top eroded to jagged spikes, sides blotched orange and yellow with lichen but still supporting a rusted latch. It marks the site of Riverside, a house long vanished, where a remarkable man once lived — his name, Henry Scotland.

Scotland was the youngest son of George Scotland, CB, Chief Justice of Trinidad, and Sarah Fergusson, only daughter of the Rev William Humphrys of the Island of Antigua, West Indies. Born in Muswell Hill, London, on 11 July 1821, he was educated at Merchant Taylor's, one of England's best public schools, and at Oxford. Admitted as a barrister in 1849, he arrived in New Zealand the following year.

Scotland practised law at New Plymouth, interested himself in politics and in 1868 was appointed to the Legislative Council.[1] He was only 45 and if the intention was to remove an independent mind from circulation the move was only partially successful. The Honourable Henry Scotland MLC became one of the last life-appointed members of the upper house and instead of dozing in his plush seat, rambling on, or absenting himself from that colonial House of Lords, he took his appointment seriously and stood as a rock of conscience in the squalid sea of a so-often greedy and ignorant settler society. And stood, and stood, for he religiously attended — and frequently spoke critically of government policy — at sessions of the Legislative Council for the next 45 years.

Scotland stood for Maori land rights, for civil liberties and, above all, for the peaceful settlement of international differences — and these were only some of

Henry Scotland
1821-1910

the concerns that put him light-years ahead of time in nineteenth century New Zealand. His name is all but forgotton on the Kaipara and the memory of only one of his causes survives. Mrs Isobel McConaughy, whose husband later owned Scotland's property (and shifted his house to the road where it later burned down), recalls that as a young woman an old Pahi resident told her that Scotland was a peculiar man. He would not allow trees to be cut down. "I suppose," she said, "he was what you would now call one of the green people."

In the Legislative Council, Scotland championed the preservation of native bush for use and ornament. He wanted not just a stop to indiscriminate cutting and burning but also protection from cattle by fencing. This outlandish refinement he justified in his scholarly way by quoting an English authority who had found that oak forests decimated by naval ship building could be saved only by keeping them free of cattle — a discovery made over a century before.[2]

Scotland's original 14-acre property on the outskirts of New Plymouth was a showcase for his beliefs. It was so outstanding that the old girls of New Plymouth Girls' High School spent a decade fund-raising to buy 10 acres of it in 1926. A school history says that Scotland had preserved the bush-clad banks of a stream as the back-drop to imaginative planting of "huge puriri trees and bluegums, with camellias and magnolias." The headmistress in 1926 made a lyrical speech:

> The avenue with its stately trees forms a worthy entrance to the beautiful grounds. The hillside curves itself into a natural amphitheatre . . . for Greek plays and dramatic pageants . . . Te Henui [the stream] the pines, the chestnuts, the native bush, array Scotlands in loveliness!

126

The property is still known as Scotlands and the grounds are regarded as the most beautiful of any girls' school in New Zealand.[3]

Scotland had to sell his New Plymouth home (worth £850 on an 1882 valuation) after suffering heavy losses in the banking collapse in the depression of the late 1880s. He moved north to a "suburbs of Pahi" 6-acre section (valued at £20 in 1882) which he had owned for many years. Riverside, his new home, was tucked away on the Pahi River but it may have seemed too close to Paparoa for the comfort of leading citizens not averse to the popular description of their town as "Gospel Gully." Scotland had recently published a pamphlet, *Denominationalism, the Bane of Christianity*, which began:

> How sickening it is to be dosed with the eternal flattering notices of Church bazaars and fancy fairs (or fayres'), organ recitals, and services of song, served up to us with almost the same regularity as our daily meals by the venal newspaper press, at the command of its lords and masters — the moneyed class — or rather that important section of it which is known as the religious world of New Zealand.

Uncompromising words for someone about to settle in a district where such activities were the staple of social life. Scotland's thesis was that Christianity would be best served without churches or ministers of religion:

> Hireling, man-made priests, with no commission from God, they hold just the same position and do the very same work as the false prophets of old. . . To look up to such men is soul-destroying delusion. The Archbishop of Canterbury or the Pope of Rome, can be no more in the eyes of God than the tohunga of the Maori or the medicine-man of the Red Indian. Jesus always discountenanced anything like the ambition of precedence among his followers. . .

The pamphlet consisted of "letters to a friend in the country" and it described how his aversion to organized religion had been expressed at a Wellington church function. He had been invited

> to put a small sum of money in this or that raffle or sweepstake, whereby, the fates being propitious, I might anon find myself the lucky possessor of some work of high art or object of everyday utility. As I was by no means ambitious of saddling myself with some miserable daub of a picture, and still less of having to carry home an embroidered smoking-cap (I am no smoker), or a pretty pair of baby's shoes (I am not a proprietor of babies), I politely declined. . . I was mean enough to do without spending a single farthing. . .[4]

If they read this pamphlet the church-centred folk of the Albertland settlements would have had at least one last laugh. Scotland was an old man when he came north, but not too old for baby's shoes. After the pamphlet was published in 1888 two sons were born to his wife Margaret, the second in 1891 when he was in his 71st year.

The view near Riverside.

Waiting for the steamer at Pahi.

Scotland's vigour was well tested by Pahi's isolation. Regular travel from the Kaipara to Wellington would have been an ordeal at any age, even after rail replaced steamer transport. A sometimes turbulent passage to Helensville, rail to Auckland, a change of trains and then coach transport over a sea of mud between bush railheads in the centre of the island (the Main Trunk was not completed until 1908) made each journey a marathon. Scotland faced these rigours for 20 years.

Some idea of the conditions he confronted is given by a question put in the Legislative Council in 1896 when he was 75:

> The Hon Mr Scotland asked the government if their attention had been called to the insecure state of the railway wharf at Helensville, Kaipara, after dark; and will the government for the safety of the public, have the said wharf lighted during such hours of the night as may be considered necessary. . .he had heard of many persons getting falls there at night. He himself had had two falls there and he never went to Helensville but he heard accounts of accidents at night. On moonlight nights, of course, there was no necessity for artificial light, but on dark nights the place was positively dangerous.[5]

With or without the moon, the issue was no light matter. "Inquiries were being made," he was told, and, if necessary, "steps would be taken."

Expecting "someone to take action," Scotland had waited six years before complaining. Local issues were not his strength. More at home, indeed assertive in matters of national or international moment, a speech the following year deflating Richard John Seddon's imperialistic posturing was a typical *tour de force* from his caustic tongue.

128

Steam and sail at the two wharves.

The premier planned to have a military detachment accompany him to Queen Victoria's diamond jubilee. Scotland warmed up slowly. Seddon might stay home and look into disquieting matters in the police department. He could concern himself with the frozen meat question, and heaps of questions of large importance to the wealth of the general population.

> I disapprove altogether of the quasi-military contingent. . .He speaks of it as a guard of honour to the premier. The Hon Sir George Whitmore says it would be a great object lesson to foreign nations. I do not know which of the foreign nations it is intended to or will intimidate. Foreign nations will have the sense to see at once that here, as in every country, there are numbers of idle people who are only too glad of the chance of getting a pleasure trip at public expense.

Scotland went on to speak of folly and glorification and the weakness colonists have for "blowing." And then:

> If any contingent is to go Home I do not see why it should be representative of brute force only. Why should thews and sinews only be represented? Why should not brain be represented too? Now, we have a great many men in this colony of brains — smart men — I defy New York to produce smarter men. Why should there not be representatives of the banking fraternity? Why should not the ex-directors of the Bank of New Zealand, and of another bank I could name, and also those of the Loan and Mercantile Agency Company — why should they not be sent? Only fancy the march past the Queen of these gentlemen, "two and two, Newgate* fashion," as Shakespeare has it, to the inspiring strains of that fine old composition known as the "Rogues' March." I think that would have a thrilling effect.[6]

* Debtors' prison, London.

Otamatea Mounted Rifles crossing a tidal inlet.

Just as well Scotland's was a life appointment. There would be no votes from Matakohe where a fireworks display and the spit-roasting of a whole ox was the accompaniment to a royal jubilee.

But soon the dispatch of military contingents became no laughing matter. In 1899 Seddon offered to send troops to South Africa — before the war against the Boers had begun. The upper house raced to endorse lower house approval. In a chamber hot with patriotism, John Rigg, former president of Wellington Trades and Labour Council, seemed the only critical voice. It was wrong, he said, to make a national issue of what was simply an attempt by private capitalists to exploit the mineral wealth of another country. The British Government was at fault. But he could not say "God defend the right" as that would destroy "the prestige of our race." It was New Zealand's duty, he declared, to uphold the great British Empire "although the cause that we engage in is not a righteous one." That was the radical opposition.

Scotland dispensed with oratory. He spoke briefly and matter-of-factly. He would help the mother country if she were in danger. But she was not. England was breaking a treaty to deprive the Boers of self-government. "I defy anybody to dispute what I say: that England is bound by treaty to respect their self-government. I very much hope even now, at this eleventh hour, that the affair will be amicably settled without any fighting at all."

"It is not our place at all to reason why," said Major Harris, normally a silent member who would not have spoken at all, "had it not been for the remarks of the Hon Mr Scotland." If the Boers did not come to their senses, "they must be wiped out of existence." He called for councillors to sing the national anthem after

130

the vote — as had happened in the other chamber the night before.

The whole council — with the exception of the old man from Pahi — moved through the "Ayes" door and on hearing the result, 36 to 1, stood and sang the national anthem and gave three cheers for the Queen.[7]

On the Kaipara the cheers echoed loudly. According to the *Farmer*, the crowd sang "Rule Britannia" at Port Albert Show after a speech of "fervid loyalty" by Richard Monk, the local MP, and the Kaipara Flats correspondent of the *Weekly News* reported that the war, "even here in the back bush' of New Zealand, lifts the toiler above the mere drudgery of ordinary commonplace existence making him feel the dignity of his nationality . . . and pride of race inherent in the heart of the British people."

At Paparoa, the Otamatea Mounted Rifles was formed. Without uniforms, in all kinds of dress and headgear, some eighty recruits hastily paraded under Captain Frank Colbeck and Lieutenants Nutsford, J.G. Coates and Douglas Cromwell Snelling. They ranged from boys (the minimum age of 17 was not observed) to old men with long and bushy whiskers and they rode a motley bunch of ponies and draught horses as well as a good number of smart hacks. As veteran H.S. McCarroll told a pioneer lunch in 1957, "the first parade was a sight one would never see again."[8]

Within a year, in the winter of 1901, fifty-odd volunteers were well enough turned out to ride to Auckland to parade before the Duke and Duchess of York. Apart from catching heavy colds in wet tents at Alexandra Park, they aquitted themselves well enough to be photographed in the *Weekly News*.

First local to enlist for overseas service was a Whakapirau stockman, J.C.W. Hills, who went away with the Rough Riders early in 1900. A year later two Maungaturoto brothers, Frank and John Hemphill, a labourer and a clerk, and two farmers, George Masson, Paparoa and William Upton, Whakapirau, went off with the 6th and 7th contingents. They were followed in 1902 by a third Hemphill brother, Harry, a clerk, and Sergeant Douglas Cromwell Snelling, farmer, both of Maungaturoto, Benjamin Birt, a Mareretu bushman, two Whakapirau farmers, James Milne and Tyrell de Labrosse, and Alexander McKenzie, a Pahi stockman. Matakohe's only volunteer, bushman Anthony

Mustering for a parade, 1913-14.

Anderson, joined the 9th contingent, which like the 10th, arrived when the Boers had already been starved to the point of surrender.

At the outbreak of war Scotland had warned that many "will lay their bones" in South Africa. He was speaking of combat, but of 6,500 New Zealanders who enlisted only seventy died in action. Accidents killed 25 and 133 died of sickness. Army bungling was more deadly than Boer bullets as the de Labrosse family found when their son Tyrell survived the short, sharp engagements of the 8th contingent only to die of sickness — with a score of others — on a scandalously mismanaged voyage home.

Scotland's opposition to the war had been explained by the *Observer* newspaper as resulting from "advanced senility." Others called him a senile traitor. The onset of the disease had been remarkably premature — he had opposed the invasion of Parihaka, New Zealand's early plans to annex Samoa and, still earlier, British repression in Ireland and India. And the disease showed no sign of remission.

In 1901 (when the mounted rifles made their arduous trek to Auckland) the symptoms surfaced as contempt for "flunkeyism and toadyism" surrounding the Duke and Duchess of York's war recruiting visit and mockery for "those beautiful arches" erected in the streets to welcome them. That year Scotland opposed the introduction of military drill into schools. It would promote fitness, supporters said, but Scotland cited Paparoa School as an example of how it would be a waste of time. His two boys at school, he told the upper house, were, "a great deal straighter in the back than I am, or ever was." And that was for the simple reason that when he was at public school he didn't have their opportunity of "strengthening my body at outdoor games."

In 1909 there was an outbreak of scorn for the "threatened honour" of a visit from Lord Kitchener who "may be the greatest strategist in the world and the greatest organizer ever known" but who had blown up the living and the dead (the grave of a Sudanese nationalist). "Do you call that heroism?"

The Legislative Council, 1910 session, found Scotland, as ever, braving a long journey, facing a Wellington winter and making speeches witty, erudite and sharply critical of what he saw about him. On 7 July he had a word for his fellow councillors:

> I think, if a cynic were to come into this chamber some afternoon and listen to one of our debates, he would be tempted to say, "Why, this is a mutual-admiration society: it's caw to me, and I'll caw to thee." "Well," another might say, "where is the harm? It is pleasant, and injures nobody." I am not so certain it does injure nobody. Sir, it is recorded by the Roman historian Tacitus that one day on leaving the Senate-house in Rome the Emperor Tiberius, after having listened to the most fulsome and most nauseating flattery of himself in the Senate-house, turned to one of his courtiers and said "Most assuredly those men were born to be slaves."

His goading did not sting a slaves' revolt against slavish following of British foreign policy. When he turned to the arms race (New Zealand had more than doubled its contribution to the goal of British naval supremacy) he spoke alone.

> I consider that the building of Dreadnoughts is the height of folly, and our contributing to those Dreadnoughts supreme folly. We were never asked to do so; it was our own act; and I think we deserve for doing so to be told that we have more money than wit. Sir, it is a

dangerous thing for England to attempt to dictate to and threaten the whole world. Even the South American republics are now having Dreadnoughts built; also France, Russia and Germany — they are all building Dreadnoughts and adding to their navies. And why? Because they can see plainly that England aspires to be the bully of the world. I am sorry to have to say it of my own country, but I firmly believe it; and it is a dangerous thing for a nation to go in for, because it must bring down a coalition against England, and that may be the end of the British Empire.

For a patrician-like figure who had expressed reservations about some of Seddon's labour legislation, Scotland welcomed surprising allies:

When I look at the Labour Party in the House of Commons, I am happy to see they have done all in their power to limit expenditure on armaments. Sir, I have great faith in the working-classes of England and in the working-classes of New Zealand: they are the untried class. As for the middle class, it is worn out; it is effete; it has had its day. Take the average middle-class Englishman out of his counting-house or from behind his counter — why, there is no more gullible individual on the face of the earth: he can be made to believe anything. . .[9]

It was a discursive speech as Scotland warned it would be. "Well, Sir," he concluded, "I cannot help getting old."

Four days later he celebrated his birthday and entered his 90th year. At mid-month he spoke against an Indecent Publications Bill. The Bible, Chaucer's *Canterbury Tales*, Shakespeare — all had "grossly indecent" passages. Are you prepared to punish the booksellers of Wellington for selling the works of Lord Byron? No one could be corrupted by a bad book who was not willing to be corrupted, he said. "I detect in this Bill just a slight suspicion of puritanical cant. I believe that the Bill, if it became law, would prove wholly inoperative. Certainly it would do no good."

The subject was a gift to a civil libertarian who loved literature and Scotland made the best of it. It was a powerful speech — and his last. Scotland died in office shortly after, on 28 July 1910, and his body made its last journey north on the long Main Trunk Line.

The *Graphic* paid tribute to his polished, thoughtful speeches and his caustic humour. A *Free Lance* obituary emphasised his independence. Scotland was "always noted for his inveterate habit of hitting out straight from the shoulder. He knew no party, and wasn't influenced in the slightest degree by what is termed the *vox populi*. He deferred to nobody but expressed outspokenly his opinions whether they happened to be popular or heretical. In fact, he rather seemed to enjoy being a party of One."

In both chambers there were eulogies, from the Prime Minister down, but as with the press, always the praise was for the form and not the substance of Scotland's message. His humanity was remembered by Wiremu Pere, of Hawkes Bay, the only Maori on the Legislative Council: "He was a white man and I a Maori, but he did not wish on that account to walk a different way from me. No; he recognized me as white as he was himself. So I regarded him as, like myself, a Maori." Pere referred to his previous experience as a member of parliament where bribes were offered, "in some cases of £100 or more." In the upper house it was different.

We have been called honourable, we are expected to act honourably, and we do so. We are not going to be influenced by money or any form of bribery. Money is filthy; money is the devil. The lawyers in some cases are the agents of the devil. They use all sorts of flattering terms in order to get money.

The Hon Dr Finlay [a lawyer] — May I suggest to the honourable gentleman that this is scarcely fitting on a motion of this kind?

The Hon Speaker [a magistrate] — I think the honourable member is not in order.

The Hon Mr Pere — The late Hon Mr Scotland was a lawyer, and he was the exception to the rule. He was a lawyer, and he was indeed a gentleman. Sir, if you live long enough you will find the truth of my words.

Pere went on to say that he felt deeply the loss of a friend. "Do not think I am going to lament in this strain for every member who may happen to die in this council; there are some I would not grieve for at all." Like Scotland, Pere knew what it was to be a minority of one:

Honourable members must not become impatient at the length of my remarks, for I am trying to express what I feel for a dear friend who has gone, and if it hurts you, or if you are annoyed at me for speaking, please do not show it. I am not afraid of you. I am alone in this Council representing my race, and I intend to be heard — one against many. Why I grieve is because I have lost the truest friend I had in the Council, and I am now looking round for a kindly face to take his place.

Centenarian Robert Sterling was present at the clearing sale of Scotland's estate. He had been to school with the two boys ("Harry and Billy each had their own pony and were always very well dressed"). He had visited the house once or twice and he particularly remembers the first occasion. "My father had sold some land to the Honourable Scotland and he sent me to ask what lawyer would be handling the matter for him. The Honourable Scotland was sitting in a big leather chair and he looked at me and laughed. Lawyer, boy? I don't need a lawyer, I make the laws."

The house was full of books and there was fine, if well-used furniture. At the sale Robert Sterling coveted a large painting over the mantelpiece. It was an early English country scene. No one bid for it. " 'I'm not allowed to give it to you,' said Billy Scotland. " 'You'll have to make some sort of payment.' So I gave him a shilling." What landscape painter the Scotlands favoured — and its true value — we shall never know. An unnoticed roof leak in the Sterling front room damaged it beyond repair.

The Scotland family dispersed. Harry, an engineer, migrated to America and Billy, an aviator, moved to Melbourne. Mrs Scotland's movements are unknown. Robert Sterling spoke to Billy in Queen Street, Auckland, before he left New Zealand. Billy had a long, loping stride and he literally bumped into his old schoolmate. Sterling remembers his quip: "What do you think you are, an aeroplane?" Billy said he had spent his inheritance but he had achieved what he wanted in aviation. He could not stay to talk, he was soon off to Australia.

The achievements of James William Humphrys Scotland, born at Pahi, educated at Paparoa Primary School (and later Kings College) made him one of the first and most distinguished pioneers of New Zealand aviation. Billy Scotland was nineteen when his father died. He went to England and gained a pilot's certificate, the second New Zealander to do so. He also flew in America and in 1913 purchased a French-built Caudron biplane and shipped it home with the intention of barnstorming the length of the country. At flying exhibitions in the major South Island cities large crowds gave him a hero's

Billy Scotland, pioneer aviator, and his Caudron biplane.

reception, the citizens of Dunedin presenting him with a gold medal for his bravery.[12]

He made the first cross-country flight in New Zealand (Invercargill to Gore, 48 miles, 20 February 1914) and a month later he set a long distance record (Timaru to Christchurch, 98 miles, average speed 47mph) that was to stay unbroken for five years. On that flight he dropped the first letter delivered by (unofficial) airmail.

At Wellington, Scotland's fearlessness was almost his undoing. The first flying exhibition had to be abandoned because of wind and to placate the impatient sensation-seeking crowd he promised to fly the next day. Conditions were hardly better but he forced his preposterous machine into the air and it crashed into tall pines at Newton Park. The plane was completely destroyed but Scotland climbed out unhurt.

A second Caudron was shipped out but it was damaged on flight trials and sold in 1915 to the Walsh brothers. Scotland contracted diptheria and although not in good health enlisted with the Royal Flying Corps. Invalided back to New Zealand after serving in the Middle East he was forced to give up his great passion and settled in Australia.

The Scotlands, father and son, were both prophets in their way and both, so far as the virtual blankness of Kaipara memory goes, without honour in their own country. For the country at large there has been honour for only one kind of courage. Henry Scotland's name appears in the 1966 three-volume *An Encyclopedia of New Zealand* — as the father of Billy Scotland, pioneer aviator. Below Billy's portrait in aviation's Hall of Fame, Auckland Museum of Transport and Technology, he is described as "son of a Kaipara farmer."

Henry Scotland, scourge of pomp and pretension, would be amused. The recognition he would want from later generations is of his ideas.

While young Gordon holds his horse, a cattle buyer (wearing topee) joins Edward and Eleanor Coates in a family photograph on Ruatuna lawn. A governess (right) is holding baby Ada.

10. The Coates family & their wayward son

Takoto e pa i runga i au mahi nunui mo te Pakeha me te Maori

(Rest, father, upon your many works for Pakeha and Maori)

-Inscription (Maori only) on Coates memorial.

Superlatives come easily to those who write of Joseph Gordon Coates, Privy Councillor, Military Cross (and Bar), the first New Zealand-born Prime Minister, "New Zealand's greatest Finance Minister" (Dr W.B. Sutch), ". . .great as a leader in government, as a statesman. . ." (Professor W.J. Gardner),[1] but this account of families settled around one small finger at the end of one arm of the multiple arms of the Kaipara must be concerned mainly with the seedbed of his career, not details of statesmanship. What family did he spring from? How was his early growth shaped?

Gordon Coates was born into a colonial reproduction of the English county scene. In dress, speech and social attitudes he was surrounded by pressures to consider himself above his neighbours. "Difficult" as a small boy, "running wild" as a young man, he cast off English inhibitions and snobbery and embraced — too enthusiastically some would say — the colonial style of life. On the male side there were three influences to react to: his father Edward's and that of his two uncles, Thomas and Henry Coates. Each, in distinctive ways, cut a dash on the early Kaipara. The brothers were descended from a long line of Herefordshire farmers, notable cattle and sheep breeders, members of the "squire-ocracy" who ran English counties before elected local government. Their father, squire of Eyton House, had thirteen children, seven of them sons — too many to share his acres. In 1866, 23-year-old Edward and his 19-year-old brother Thomas left for New Zealand. Henry came later. Travelling in a three-masted clipper's spacious saloon (it was half empty, an army officer and a lawyer were the only others who could afford the cost), they reached Auckland in just under four months.[2]

The fare in the *Winterthur* had been paid by Washington Charters, owner of the Ulster Linen Company, Belfast, who had married the oldest Coates daughter. He also financed the brothers' land purchases. The Belfast linen mills, notorious for their conditions of labour, were some of the most profitable in mid-century industrial Britain. The brothers had corresponded with Francis Hull, son of another rich Belfast millowner, who had settled on the Otamatea five years before. While spying out the land they stayed for several months in his three-storey house built on the lower slopes of Pukekororo.

On one expedition they rowed up the Arapaoa to Metcalfe's Clairmont and walked back along the beach towards Hukatere. They reached a small mangrove-fringed inlet, packed their clothes on their heads, and swam across. They climbed a low cliff, stood upon easy rolling country and saw good soil supporting light virgin bush. It was the 2500 acre Unuwhao block — land, in a phrase from the Coates family history, "originally granted to the Maoris in 1866 by Sir George Grey." Francis Hull had bought it from the Maori owners, resold 80 acres to C.J. Metcalfe and was pleased to let the Coates brothers buy the rest.

The brothers lived for six years in a four-roomed cottage closer to the water than present-day Ruatuna. They called it Eyton, after the mansion at home. Then in 1873, although remaining in farming partnership with Edward, Thomas married and moved down river to the Te Kawau block. He had bought it in 1871 from Manukau, the Uriohau chief, for £150. On a commanding headland with distant harbour views, one side looking over the water to Pahi, the other across mangroves to Manukau's village of Karakanui, he built a substantial shingle-roofed kauri house with attic bedrooms.

Elizabeth Phillips of Sudley House, Gloucestershire, married Thomas in St Mary's Cathedral, Parnell, and in thirteen years at Te Kawau bore him six of their eight children. Four were born in the first four years, only two surviving infancy. Thomas and Elizabeth moved from Te Kawau in 1886 when they bought the 3000-acre Pukekororo block, near Kaiwaka, for its kauri timber. They lived there for ten years before making their final home on a stud farm on 300 acres of Maori leasehold at what is now the Auckland suburb of Orakei.

The prospect of profit from milling was not the only reason for the shift from the river. Thomas, like his brother, gave musical items at Pahi concerts — he

Thomas Coates.

An early view of Ruatuna, imported stud cattle — breeding stock strictly unavailable to other farmers — in foreground.

was a violinist and bass singer — but unlike his brother he failed to fit into the life of the Kaipara community. There was a fierceness to the stylish cut of his whiskers and it was an accurate portrayal of his temperament. He was squire material, one to relish clattering into the village on a spirited horse, the bystanders forced aside, the bridle thrown to a lackey. Waiting for tides, bending to the oars, dragging a rowboat through salt mud — how very different the entry into Pahi settlement. His autocratic ways received without enthusiasm in the wider world, the Coates appetite for command was restricted to the circle of his own family.[3] His sons, sapped of initiative, failed to make any mark. His brother's sons, Rodney and Gordon, were to be the sole public figures of the next generation.

Thomas Coates retained ownership of Te Kawau. Its eleven acres of fruit trees were leased to George Haines, the Pahi storekeeper. (Haines accidentally shot himself in the orchard when clubbing a wild pig with the butt of a loaded gun.) A remnant of Maori land, a 10-acre waterfront piece, site of a headland pa, was added in 1907, purchased for £30 from Mihaka Makoare of Pouto, but the whole property remained unoccupied. On one of the finest sites on the Kaipara the house stood open to wind and rain for decades. Derelict, with a dangerous staircase, it was barely usable for one son's camping honeymoon in 1922 and for years the neglected orchard came alive only when Pahi opportunists made it the location of carefully timed picnics. The house finally collapsed in the wind and there was no trace of habitation when the Te Kawau block was sold for soldier settlement after World War Two.

139

Today the old house site is marked by Norfolk Island pines, a semi-circle of oaks, a distinctive monkey puzzle and a grand Moreton Bay fig. At the end of the headland, just below the trees, can be found the gravestone of the first child, Thomas, born 5 February 1874, died at 13 months. The third daughter, Fanny Jassmine, born 15 July 1877, died at 18 months, is also recorded on the stone. It was entirely in character for a patriarchal Victorian not to mark a daughter's death — and it was not. The inscription below baby Thomas's name has been added in recent times.[4]

Edward Coates was still a bachelor when his younger brother fathered his fourth child. He rectified the matter that year. Guns fired at Pahi and bonfires blazed on promontories reaching into the Arapaoa when he brought his city bride, Eleanor Aickin, to the splendid new house he had prepared half way between Pahi and Matakohe. After passing the Funnel, the couple had travelled for two hours in sight of land the brothers had been farming for 10 years. For 10 miles (16km) as the tern flies, they had passed the Komiti block, the Hukatere block, the Unuwhao block — most of the Tinopai Peninsula, over 25,000 acres, leasehold and freehold, in Coates hands.

Ruatuna, their waiting home, sited on high ground back from the water, was built by Samuel Cooksey with the same craftsman's respect for wood as he had shown in building the vaulted roof of Pahi Hall. Externally a conventional colonial house, Ruatuna's interior lines soared to follow the high gable roof. With no ceiling, gable-end windows normally servicing attic bedrooms gave top-light to a generous farm kitchen and a comfortable living room. Modest lean-tos served as bedrooms. Edward Coates had modelled the plan on a Scottish hunting lodge he had visited and Cooksey lovingly put it into effect. A cornet player and fine tenor singer, Edward had been impressed by the acoustics of the lodge.[5] Not just that fact and nostalgia had dictated the design. Over six feet tall like his brother, he would have ill-fitted the low ceilings, stunted doorways (and thigh pinching tables) typical of many first homes of immigrants from ill-fed industrial Britain.

Eleanor Kathleen Aickin and Edward had been married in St Lukes Church, Mt Albert, Auckland on 28 May 1877 and on 3 February 1878 a child was born. He was named Joseph Gordon — and the boy impatient to start life stormed on as lustily for the next 65 years. Gunshots had given his mother a district's welcome, the gun-carriage of a state funeral were to give her son the farewell of a nation.

Coates was born to the idea of public office. His father sat on the bench at Pahi court hearings, he was trustee of hall and cemetery, his guiding hand was on school and church. He was in charge at early regattas and when the North Kaipara Agriculture Association held its first show at Pahi in 1876 he was, at 33, its first president. Genuine popularity, not just deference to the gentry, had lit the welcoming bonfires for his bride. A squire's obligation to serve carried with it an edge of superiority but, unlike Thomas, Edward did not let the edge cut too deeply. It was a wise precaution as the hostile reaction to organization of a concert that followed the 1876 regatta shows. A *Weekly News* correspondent was outraged by old world social distinction. A crowd of all ages and sexes had been kept waiting nearly an hour, he said, before the concert doors were opened.

> I ascertained that it was always the same at Pahi, the front seats being reserved for a few favourites . . . who were later admitted by a side door. As all paid alike this conduct on the part of the managers reflects the greatest discredit and deserves the censure of the public. As far as I could see and understand, there were quite as delicate ladies and children outside . . . as any of those for whom the front seats had been reserved.

But some democrats exacted crude retribution. They persisted in talking in loud voices when Edward Coates's "first class singing deserved breathless silence."[6]

Edward did not escape his origins and in later years hoped to move to a society more exalted than that of the Kaipara. A letter written in 1896 to Washington Charters, his brother-in-law in Ireland, reveals a desire to follow Thomas Coates's example:

> Tomorrow my boy Gordon and myself go over to Tom (who is leaving with the family for his Auckland farm) to help him pack up. . . Tom still holds the Pukekororo farm, employing a man to manage it, but will live mostly at the Auckland place. I am pleased as Tom's girls were simply 'buried alive' at Pukekororo. No society fit for them. . . It is my intention to do likewise when I have a few pounds in hand, but it is hard to make headway with present low prices for stock. My boys could manage here and I could help them at busy times.[7]

Edward's daughters Ada and Dolly, who did not marry, may have lived different lives if, like their cousins, they too had moved to a society "fit for them." But the shift from Ruatuna was never made. Edward had suffered from recurring bouts of a mental illness and the attacks worsened. What local legend says was the result of being bitten by a dog has been more precisely described as either

Henry Coates.

Easy to identify. Gordon and Rodney Coates with the shearing gang.

"melancholia," a deep depression, or "asthenia," an anxiety neurosis. The illness finally incapacitated him and he died in 1905 aged 61. His wife Eleanor outlived him by thirty years.

For Gordon Coates, "society" standards were always maintained. His father (and his Uncle Thomas) had dressed for the farm in a white shirt, butterfly collar, knotted tie, and half top hat. Gordon and his brother Rodney turned out for mustering wearing silk shirts, ties and bowler hats. Only the bowler came off for shearing. His sisters, of course, dressed as ladies should and did not attend the local school, being educated by a succession of governesses (it was a rapid succession until Eleanor intervened in her husband's appointments to require teaching merit ahead of looks). And around Ruatuna, peacocks strutted, grape arbours ripened, and — echo of the game park — a herd of alpaca, a kind of llama with a valuable coat of hair, swivelled their stately, spittle-aiming heads.

Sadly, the gracious life was taken to caricature on the neighbouring 480-acre farm settled by a late arrival, the Coates's older brother Henry. He built a bachelor cottage on top of what is now known as Uncle Harry's Hill and tunnelled into its slopes to build stables and kennels for a pack of hounds that ran to the echo of his hunting bugle. His scarlet tunic flashing across Kaipara bush-burn and bracken fern was a spectacle that produced mixed feelings. Henry Scotland, for one, the legislative councillor who lived down river, was later to demand that blood sports be kept out of New Zealand.

An accomplished rider, Henry Coates owned a show horse of some renown and regularly invited the district to hurdle races on his property — races he

142

Wool away! Thumb in lapel, Gordon Coates supervises.

invariably won. He was not unaware of the figure he cut. Presiding over the carving of a whole roast bullock at Matakohe's royal jubilee celebrations in 1887, he declared with sly humour that his bachelor skills were "naturally limited." But he was willing to change status given a chance and he hoped "some lady might take pity on his lonely condition." Tolerated eccentricity turned sour when Henry's wonder horse was trained to knock on doors. An urgent hoof thudding on the kitchen door at breakfast time and the rebuke, "Ella, your smoke was up late this morning," was the least of the crosses Eleanor Coates had to bear. Imperious in the saddle, Uncle Harry performed his circus trick at all hours, day or night, to summon attendance on his wants. There was a sigh of relief when, in old age, he returned to Herefordshire. His last days were spent roaming the countryside evangelizing.[8]

Uncle Harry back in England.

With responsibilities greater than bachelor Harry — seven times greater not counting wife and governess: there were seven children — Edward Coates sweated in his white silk shirts and his hunting bugle was not for idle diversion. He had warred with packs of wild dogs (the last of the Maori kuri)[9] and with hordes of wild pigs before the bush and scrub and fern of the Tinopai Peninsula could be stocked, and once it was only his habit of carrying the bugle that saved him from a savage boar when his call for help was heard in time.

Gordon and Rodney plunged into the same forbidding country in weeks-long musters of semi-wild cattle. Domesticated stock were circulated as decoys and gaucho-style riders wrestled young bulls to the ground for castrating and branding. In such a foray into the bush Gordon broke a leg when his horse fell on him. His young sister Ada recalled in later years the sound of sawing and hammering she heard in the night when Gordon reached home and his father made splints to set a broken thigh. It was over a week before Gordon received medical attention and the doctor who reset the break failed to ensure a satisfactory mend.[10] On the platform, Gordon Coates always orated with one leg forward — an emphatic stance, but one due not so much to passionate conviction as to the fact that that leg was longer than the other.

In another accident on a remote part of the farm a falling tree pinned a worker by the arm. Help could not be reached in time, the tree could not be moved. Gordon Coates took a knife and freed the man by cutting his arm off. He reached hospital alive but did not survive the ordeal. The dead man's family, the Liddles of Te Kopuru, were always grateful that by Coates's action their son had at least been given a chance of survival. Years later, Harry Liddle, a descendant who heard of the accident as a child, had the story confirmed in unusual circumstances. He was travelling near Orewa when a large car veered across the road and crashed into him. The driver brushed aside the problem with offers of a taxi to wherever the young man was going, a tow for his car, and all expenses met. It was Prime Minister Coates, in notably expansive mood for a work-day afternoon, and hearing the name Liddle, he recalled that so much more sobering accident from his sterner days in the bush.[11]

Gordon Coates's mother provided another strand to the physical strength and practical sense that he owed to his farming forebears. Eleanor Coates was the daughter of Dr Thomas Aickin, highly qualified (Dublin and Berlin) superintendent of Avondale Mental Hospital. He was a grandson of Dr James Patten, surgeon on Cook's second voyage in the *Resolution*, and tales of a climate where it was possible "to sleep under hedgerows" are said to have attracted him to New Zealand.

Eleanor's mother, like her father an Anglo-Irish Protestant, was a Casement. A nephew was Casement Aickin, prominent Auckland surgeon, and Sir Roger Casement, knighted for distinguished services up the Amazon and in Africa, was a cousin with whom she corresponded. Roger Casement took up the cause of Irish independence and in 1916, the year Gordon Coates enlisted for active service, he was hanged for treason, his body cast into quicklime. The British government had made much of his homosexuality to counter influential calls from around the world for a reprieve.

Bleak terrain. Mrs. Hinks, housekeeper on Pukehuia, the Jenkins farm at Marohemo, gathers greenery, 1917.

Perhaps it was this Anglo-Irish intellectual inheritance that made the infant Gordon Coates a great trial to his mother. Certainly active curiosity had him wandering far afield — even after a horse's hoof quite severely injured his mouth (the permanently disfigured upper lip was later covered by a moustache). By the time he was three it required a Maori woman in full-time employment to supervise his explorations. Scarcely amenable material for a governess, he was sent to Matakohe School, but a three-mile row and a mile long walk along a bush track gave well-exploited opportunities for truancy. Sketchy formal schooling ended before he reached standard six. Some tuition from an English cadet on the neighbouring Adams farm hardly remedied deficiencies that handicapped him throughout his career.

Coates compensated for lack of education with assertiveness laid over an inborn skill in handling people. A combination of charm and bluster, if you like. Geoffrey Webster, a veteran journalist who observed him closely during the depression years, put it this way: "A man 'with a way with him'. . .he had a built-in swagger, was fond of glaring at people, and thrived on strife."[12]

The young Coates threw himself into local activities. At 22 he joined the Otamatea Mounted Rifles, at 27 he was a member of the Otamatea County Council and president (like his father before him) of the North Kaipara Agricultural Association. Command of the volunteers and chairmanship of the county followed — the county chair being later taken by his brother Rodney for 27 years. The mould of the worthy English squire seemed unbroken. And perhaps it was, given the truth of English nursery rhymes about milkmaids.

The Prime Minister speaking in 1928. Maui Pomare, G. S. Anderson and Downie Stewart in the front row.

Coates was physically attractive. Smart riding breeches, jaunty buttonhole, hat rakishly angled, he appears in photographs as a dashingly eligible bachelor. But despite social pressures he was not drawn to the marriageable products of Victorian households who sang at regatta's end, "Come where the moonbeams linger. . ." It was the warm spontaneity of his Maori neighbours' daughters that he favoured.*

Centenarian Robert Sterling recalls that "Gordon Coates always seemed to dance with Maori girls." He remembers the military ball held at Paparoa to mark the opening of the Drill Hall. Top brass from Wellington were present. There was a belle-of-the-ball, a Whakapirau settler's attractive daughter, and the beau was — who else? — Lieutenant J.G. Coates. But the beau declined to partner the belle. Coates was very angry when some troopers dragged him on to the dance floor — there was some talk of assault on a superior officer — and he left the hall.[13]

By 1911, when at the age of 33 he entered parliament, there was abundant proof of his preference. An early liaison involved the daughter of Te Mate Manukau, the Arapaoa chief, and his wife, the former Maraea Rogan. Children were born and in the marry-our-daughters tradition of the Gittos era, land was given. Ngati Whatua elders recall great bitterness when the prospect of nuptials faded but the land above the Ruawai flats seaward of Rogan's Hill was retained. Mohi Manukau, grandson of Te Mate, even speaks of tar-and-feathers talk when he was a boy. There was a flicker of compensation years later when one of the offspring appeared in Whangarei Court and asked her name, replied, "Coates."[14]

Annie Ngapo, daughter of a farm worker at Ruatuna, Hohepa Hemi Ngapo, also bore Gordon Coates's children. May, whose baptism certificate gives the

---

* An early courtship of a Pakeha, a Hukatere school teacher, ended when her father forbade marriage into a family he considered tainted by mental instability. This blow is said to be the reason why Coates "ran wild". The teacher never married and when Gordon died gave Rodney a posy to put on his grave.

146

address, Ruatuna, was born in 1906 and a second child, Rawinia, followed. Coates took no part in their upbringing. Annie Ngapo later married and in the customary way, her first family was raised by the grandparents. Rawinia died when she was two or three years old and the mother died of influenza when she was 32.

In effect orphaned at ten, May recalls her girlhood as an utterly miserable one. "I was not brought up, but dragged up," she says, and poorly educated, had to take live-in domestic jobs from an early age. She married at 18 while working at Te Kopuru hospital and apart from once having to search for a birth certificate (for a holiday passport) the painful Kaipara was put completely behind her. Looking back through an album showing the warm family life of her marriage, one dim photograph of a woebegone little girl with thin, rickety legs is the sole connection with the past.[15]

In 1911 the Kaipara electorate wanted a man of action. Seddon's Liberal Party which had done so much for small farmers had grown stale. Opposing the sitting Liberal member, John Stallworthy, were candidates Coates and Field. Standing as Independent Liberal, Coates declared he would give the government one session to make changes. Failing results he would vote with the opposition. Field was in outright opposition. By today's vote counting Coates lost his first election. Stallworthy polled 2301 votes, Coates 1843 and Field 848. By the electoral law then in force, the top candidate's failure to gain an overall majority required a second ballot. Coates won all of Field's support and was returned by 2744 votes to Stallworthy's 2172.

As promised, Coates supported the government at a crucial vote on 27 February 1912, but failing its last chance to reform, at three in the morning of 6 July he voted to bring it down. A moribund Liberal Party that could not deliver was replaced by "Reform" conservatives who could — for a time. And Coates soon proved that the right had recruited not just another party hack. One of his first successes was to end the delays which always seemed to follow Maori applications for a pension, one of his biggest triumphs was to help lift from gumdiggers' backs the system of servitude that shopkeepers and gum merchants had imposed.

Speaking to a bill he had amended to ensure that diggers received the true value of their gum he said:

> If there is one thing the gum merchants do not want it is this bill. This is the first time that a government has taken sufficient interest in the gumdigger to even consider his claims in parliament and the effect of such interest will be that the merchants will find that the business will be run on different lines than it has been in the past.[16]

State intervention on behalf of what he called "the ordinary cockatoo" followed. He put a stop to syndicates buying up Maori land for resale to farmers. On the figures he put before parliament the intervention was not before time:

> I know of land bought at 10/- to 25/- per acre which in about three years has been sold at £6 per acre. Not only has the Native been exploited to the extent of the difference between 10/- and £6 but the settler who has gone on that land. . .has to pay interest on the money which has gone into the pockets of the speculator.[17]

Other radical policies were to tax large estates, to assist timber workers become farmers and to nationalise the liquor and tobacco trades. Electorally popular most of his causes may have been, but Coates was no demagogue looking for any bandwagon, as one wartime episode showed. Real and concocted reports of German atrocities brought calls for retaliation against New Zealanders of real or imagined German descent. Dalmatians who had migrated to escape military service from the Austro-Hungarian empire occupying their country were among the targets. Windows were broken, individuals were persecuted, the German sausage was renamed. Ignorance and hysteria did not bypass the Kaipara and Fritz Rathbone of Whakapirau, young son of a German mother, was prudently renamed Fred.

In 1916, at the height of the ugly campaign, Gordon Coates kept his head as this parliamentary exchange shows:

> *Coates:* I know people of German birth who are as loyal as anyone could possibly be. . .They are industrious and hardworking. . . *Wilford:* By the cables tonight the Germans are putting our fellows to work, and pretty hard too. *Coates:* That is true but why should two wrongs make a right?. . . There is absolutely no argument why we should do the same. *Wilford:* It is the only way to stop them. It is the only thing they will understand. *Coates:* That is not the way. . . I do not agree with persecuting them for the purpose of giving them a taste of what their country is doing. I will not be a party to that.

Later in his speech Coates defended the "Austrians" on the gumfields.

> *Coates:* We have difficulty in the north in connection with the Dalmatians. The question has come before the House on several occasions. I say the majority of them are loyal to Great Britain and the Allies. . . *Wilford:* How do you know who are loyal and who are not? *Coates:*There are dozens of these men whom I know to be loyal — men to whom I would trust my life. There are others for whom I would not give tuppence but that is another matter. . . The majority of these men on the gumfields could be trusted. . .[18]

As so often happens, it was the armchair patriots who were fiercest. (One, indeed, had been fierce enough to send a white feather to Coates and had been pulled off his horse and whipped for his trouble.)[19] In 1914, at the age of 36, Coates had married Marguerite Grace Coles, a London doctor's daughter who was waitressing in Dargaville, and the first of five daughters had been born, but within months of his plea for tolerance he volunteered for active service. He fought in some of the bloodiest battles of the war and was several times wounded and twice decorated. He rose no higher in rank than major because, it was said, he put the welfare of his men first.

Coates was demobilized to take cabinet rank and within six years was Prime Minister. In one three-year term he initiated a state housing project, gave municipalities control over public transport and introduced family allowances — and these were only some of the reforms that outraged private enterprise hardliners. The child allowance for low income families of 2/- (20c) per week, per child — with provision for illegitimate children "in some cases" — was also derided by the Labour opposition for its paltriness, but it introduced a principle said to be in effect nowhere else in the world. Coates retained his Native Affairs portfolio and again broke new ground. A politician with knowledge of the language was rare indeed. With leaders like Apirana Ngata (whom he knighted although in opposition) and Te Puea Herangi ("Princess" Te Puea) Coates established a close working relationship. Compensation was paid for confiscated land and Maori culture was fostered.

Headstrong, a novice in the big league, with a raw energy that had him ploughing up and down the public baths near parliament every morning, a countryman's sturdy confidence was carrying his policies through. It was the brash confidence that made senior New Zealand public servants wince when he strode into a London meeting of heads of state singing out (from a popular tune) "The Gangs All Here! — the kind of assurance that back at home bothered visitors when he smoked cigars during meals. Plunged out of depth by the depression, he needed more than confidence to cope with disaster. Early in office, inexperience had made him trusting of incompetent officials — one decrepit minder of prime ministers since Seddon even botched arrangements for an audience at Buckingham Palace — but now, as Minister of Finance desperately floundering for solutions, he reached beyond the encrusted bureaucracy to recruit his own brains trust. He chose brilliant young graduates

Plumed for the palace

10 Downing Street, right, with Sir Francis Bell.

well outside establishment thinking. Trips back to the farm were frequently made with three young men in tow, Horace Belshaw, Dick Campbell and Bill Sutch — all left-wing economists, Belshaw moderately so, Campbell quite definitely, and Sutch definitely indeed. For a senior minister in a conservative government, an unlikely trio.[20]

Coates made his brother's house his Kaipara headquarters and the brains trusters spent weekends around the kitchen table sparking against each other's ideas. Shirley Tonkin, Rodney's daughter, remembers them arguing into the night. Her uncle carefully listened. Against powerful opposition the exchange rate was raised, interest rates were reduced, there was mortgage relief, and when the trading banks failed to co-operate, the Reserve Bank was set up to monitor their actions.

No measures could now save Coates's reputation. Impatient dismissal of the unemployed had earned him life-long enemies. As one biographer writes, "Men did not appreciate being told brusquely to 'hike out into the country' to look for work when they were expecting sympathy."[21] The answer to a request for an extra dole payment, the phrase thrown out in a hotel, "I'll see them eating grass first," has gone into folklore.[22]

Callous responses to the misery of the depression generated intense reactions beyond the relief camps. One election day a group of Helensville mill workers made the long launch journey to Matakohe just to ensure that Coates — still the popular local boy — did not get a 100 per cent vote.[23] A rhyme still remembered around the Kaipara by those who were children at the time has a Grimms' story book savagery:

> Oh lord above, send down a dove,
> With wings as sharp as razors,
> To cut the throats of Forbes and Coates
> For cutting back our wages.

On another level, the peccadillos of his private life, real and imagined, were the subject of deep interest. As one historian puts it, "He became the centre of more slanderous rumours than any other New Zealand politician except Seddon." Particularly persistent were tales of his alleged promiscuity. They were so hurtful to the family that at one period a private detective was hired to trace his movements. He was shadowed for several months with negative results.

Coates's use of alcohol, about standard for the ex-rugby player, racegoing New Zealand male that he was, became exaggerated to alcoholism by detractors. Some supporters went to the other extreme of denying his drinking habits. The electorate knew him simply as "one of the boys" — one indeed known to have difficulty reversing his car after social functions. An old war comrade, Ken Smithyman, who was secretary of the Te Kopuru Labour Party, used to put aside politics to perform the task for him.[24] "The RSA boys" would have enjoyed the statement of Sir Bernard Ashwin, secretary to the Treasury when Coates was Minister of Finance. He said that plausibility was given to vicious rumours "by the fact that he had a very ruddy complexion and, from war injuries, was sometimes a little uncertain in his gait."[25]

Perhaps more to the point was the close relationship Coates had with the

A blacksmith sharpens stonemasons' tools at an argillite outcrop on the Coates property.

liquor trade. The man who had been elected to office advocating nationalisation of that trade became, in the words of Eliot Davis, brother of the brewery knight, Sir Ernest Davis, "one of the greatest stalwarts who fought for the trade in parliament."[26] As we shall see, his work was not forgotten.

Some other fall-out from the rumour-mill vastly amused Kaipara residents. One visitor to Matakohe looked about, and much puzzled, asked, "Where's the railway station?" He took some convincing that the nearest station (Maungaturoto) was many miles away.[27] Coates, as Minister of Railways, had not looped the line to his own farm gate. Another visitor came equipped with the surprising knowledge that the long drive into Ruatuna was lined with ornamental cast-iron light standards — all ex-railway of course.[28] Letters preserved at Ruatuna show that, in fact, Thomas Coates had pressed to have the line diverge through his Pukekororo property so that he could quarry building stone at Bald Rock. Uncle Tom, always on a short fuse, exploded in incredulous anger at his nephew's failure to co-operate.[29]

Coates's personal attitude to money was not one that suggested an appetite for corruption. He put little value on it. It was for splashing on entertainment or distributing in generous handouts to old war comrades fallen on hard times. His cavalier indifference to expenditure produced a situation in the family partnership where Rodney could sign cheques on his own authority but Gordon was required to have his brother co-sign them.[30] So much for the Minister of Finance's signature down on the farm.

Coates with daughters Barbara and Sheila, 1934.

Coates's own wife and five daughters lived in make-and-mend frugality, putting on heroic appearances for frequent short-notice visits by important guests. (There was something heroic, too, about the five daughters' duties at election time. Together with Rodney's two daughters they made a formidable seven-woman electoral team — turned loose on country dances with instructions never to refuse a dance.) It is a reflection of the financial constraints they laboured under that when Mrs Coates, a cabinet minister's wife, received hospital treatment during World War II, she tipped her nurse threepence — an action resented as much for its inappropriateness as for its extreme parsimony.[31]

When in 1935 Coates lost office, and with it his ministerial house, his sisters Ada and Dolly continued to occupy Ruatuna, the family home — after all, with brother Rodney, they had kept the farm going for a very long time. A testimonial meeting in his honour attended by over 2000 supporters at Dargaville presented him with funds to build another house on the farm.[32] A Public Works cottage was extended and a dormitory wing added for the five girls. Now called Eyton, it was then named by the family, with some accuracy, The Dump. Mohi Manukau, one of the builders, has vivid recollections of conversations where Coates raised the subject of the Maori land he had been given years before in expectation of him marrying Mohi's aunt. The matter had worried him and he had wondered how the land could be given back. "He suggested that if I married one of his daughters he could leave the land in his will to her and in that way it would be returned to the Manukau family. I was willing, and so was the daughter, but Mrs Coates — she was an Englishwoman — she vetoed the idea."[33]

152

Genuine offer or cynical ploy, whatever the interpretation of this unlikely episode, when in 1943 Coates died suddenly in office as a non-party War Minister in the Labour Cabinet, and then Rodney died not long after, the land was so heavily mortgaged that a succession of death duties forced the sale of all but the 360-acre Ruatuna block. Eleven years in local politics and thirty-three years in national politics had left the nest conspicuously unfeathered.

Coates was a thwarted liberal fallen into ruthless company. Picked out when his war record brought reflected glory to his party he was dropped when his colleagues wanted to distance themselves from the depression. The statesman remade as scapegoat. Ironically, free of his former friends when they deserted the war cabinet, he remained in the cabinet to cap his career with honour and largely rehabilitated himself in the eyes of the public.

On his death, the quality of Coates's human gifts were nowhere better demonstrated than by the grief of that considerable Waikato leader, Te Puea Herangi. Unable to have his body lie in state at Turangawaewae for a day, as she wanted, she organized a Maori reception for it at St Mary's Church, Parnell, and travelled to Matakohe for the burial. When the memorial church to Gordon Coates was opened at Matakohe in 1950, Te Puea made a second pilgrimage north to lay a sprig of red manuka on his grave.[34]

The ambivalence in the public and private life of Gordon Coates is expressed by another memorial, one erected at the foot of the Brynderwyns where the road to Dargaville turns off from Highway One. It carries in bronze the Maori inscription translated at the head of this chapter and in English gives the salute "Farmer, Soldier, Statesman — He was Indeed a Man." Built of granite blocks from a demolished London bridge, it stands bleakly in a carpark — perhaps not inappropiately, since it is the tribute of a brewer. It is the anonymous tribute of Sir Ernest Davis to the politician who was once going to have the state take over his business.

Over another jump, Paparoa Show.

A note on sources

Around the river, paper has not fared better than the trees it is made from. The disappearance of the Coates papers entrusted to Dr. Sutch (note 1, chapter 10) is only the latest episode in a sorry saga. At Paparoa, the *Albertlander* papers of the scholarly storekeeper, Henry Hook, held in safekeeping after his death, were tossed out of an upstairs window on a wet day by a child; at Whakapirau the Jackman records were systematically burned; at Matakohe, John Isbister's considerable collection was preserved by one relative, only to be destroyed by another; and at Pahi, the voluminous Chadwick records of the mill, general store and water transport were stored in the attic of the beachfront house until the 1950 s when they were loaded into a dinghy by an ageing daughter and night after night rowed into the harbour and dumped. That Otamatea County Council recently lost portraits of all its chairmen by storing them on soil under the floor of its offices is par for the course.

Abbreviations: AJHR *(Appendices of the Journals of the House of Representatives);* AWN *(Auckland Weekly News);* PD *(Parliamentary Debates);* NZF *(New Zealand Farmer);* NZH *(New Zealand Herald)*

(1)   THE FATAL COMPACT
1.   In recent years the bust has been stored in Whare Maori, the "Devil's House", at Ratana Pa; it is now held on deposit in Auckland Museum for the Otamatea Marae.
2.   Simmons, Whakairo, 1986.
3.   Family history, typescript, Murray Gittos, Auckland.
4.   *Missionary Register,* 1843, p423.
5.   George Graham ms., private collection.
6.   Mabett, *Wellsford — Tidal Creek to Gum Ridge,* 1968.
7.   Byrne, *The Riddle of the Kaipara,* 1986.
8,9.   Turton, *Maori Deeds of Land Purchases,* 1878.
10.   *Albertland Gazette,* 1-9-1863.
11.   Butler, *this Valley in the Hills,* 1963.
12.   Hovey Brookes, in *the Albertlanders.*
13.   *AJHR,* 1861, C1.
14.   Being restored by Trevor and Chrissie Linnell.
15.   Manuscript, AIM.
16.   "Maoris and the Navy" by J. C. (James Cowan), clipping, 5-6-1928. The New Zealand squadron was not excepted even in modern times and Cowan wrote: "One would have imagined the Maoris were sufficiently British in nationality . . . to be permitted to enter the navy for which they help to pay."
17.   Simmons, *op cit.*
18.   James Wilson survey, 1858. He was trained by his father "a Maori scholar of knowledge and understanding far beyond the average". (Furkert, *NZ*

Engineers). Tutaimakanoa, or Pangatutai as it was shown on Wilson's map, was called Karepo (sea grass) when it was sold — to wipe away the earthiness no doubt.
19.   Best, *Maori Religion and Mythology,* part 1.
20.   See Butler for other resolutions.
22.   Hay, *Brighter Britain,* 1882.
23.   Brett and Hook, *the Albertlanders,* 1927.
24.   Gittos history. See *NZF,* October, 1896, for letter on beekeeping by Marianne Gittos.
25.   *AWN,* 22-4-1882.
26.   "Two Young Ladies Horse Whip a Surveyor at Kaipara", clipping, nd, Thayer Fairburn, Titirangi.
27.   *AWN,* 22, 29/4, 6-5-1882.
28.   *NZH,* 11-7-1882.
29.   Interview Thayer Fairburn, his nephew.
30.   Hurndall diary, quoted by Butler.
31.   Scott, *Ask That Mountain,* 1975.
32.   Henderson, *Ratana,* 1963.
33.   Interview, Ned Wiapo, Whangarei.
34.   Interview, Sir Graham Latimer, Taipuha.

(2)   SCHEMES AND DREAMS
1, 8, 10. "A Trip to the Kaipara Settlements", *AWN,* 15-12-1886.
2.   *AWN,* 24-1-1880.
3.   Reprinted *Northern Advocate,* 7-2-1976.
4, 5.   *PD,* 25-11-1879, 17-8-1880.
7.   *Lily, Minnie Casey, Durham, Kena, Tongariro, City of Cork.*
9.   Linton typescript, Max Wilson, Paparoa.
11.   Butler, op cit.
12, 13. *NZH,* 9-2-1884, 17-1-1885.
14.   *Mahinga O Te Tupeka,* na Hone Waiti.
15, 17. *NZF,* February 1887 p50.
16 19. *AWN,* 19-2, 2-4, 7-5, 4-6-1887.
20.   *As Old as Auckland,* 1984.
21 24. Recollections Luther Hames, 1922,

typescript, Stella Fenwick, Pahi.

22. Scott, *Fire on the Clay;* Lambert, *Pottery in New Zealand;* Reynolds "The Colonial Potteries of James Wright", *Historic Places,* March 1985.

23. "An Artist in Pottery", *AWN,* 30-3-1878.

25. *AWN,* 24-1-1880.

26. "Legends of the Kaipara", 7pp handwritten verse, of which this is one page. Lila Pheasant, Auckland.

(3) *THE GREAT PAHI REGATTA*

1. Minute book 1910-18, OKM.

2. Held by John Linnell, Tamworth, N.S.W.

3, 5. *AWN,* 29-6-1878; 7-2-1880; Reischek, *Yesterdays in Maoriland.*

7. "Matakohe Memories", typescript, 21pp, OKM.

8, 9. *Weekly Herald,* 3, 10-6-1876.

10, 11. *NZH* 22-11, 5-12,1884.

(4) *HE MADE THE VINE FLOURISH*

1. Identified in copy held by Mavis Bull. Those not named in this chapter are: Dandy Jack (H. McMurdo); The Fiend (Frank Jackman);The Mayor (George Haines); Pirate (Captain Rawson); The Member (Lewis Rye).

2. Interviews with grandchildren, Mavis Bull and William Jackman and great grandson Warren Butterworth, all of Auckland.

3. Report by P. W. Barlow, rewritten (to its detriment) for his *Kaipara, Experiences of a Settler in Northern New Zealand,* 1888.

4. Hay, *Brighter Britain,* pp109, 244-52.

5. *New Zealander,* 4-5-1861; *Southern Cross,* March, 1875; *AWN,* 27-3-1876.

6. By Du Breuill, Reemelin, and Thudicum and Dupres. See Scott, *Winemakers of New Zealand.*

7. Gittos family history.

8. Interview, Joy Aickin, Matakohe.

9. Butler, *This Valley in the Hills.*

10. *Annual Report,* Dept. Ag., 1907, pp238, 245.

11. *NZ Graphic,* 15-12-1900.

13. "Vine Culture for Winemaking in NZ" by "Scilicet", *NZF,* May 1902, pp225-6.

14. *NZF,* April 1902, pp170-4.

15. George Graham clipping, nd, private scrapbook: "One impious person, having an idea only as to how to make money, converted his flour mill (no longer a payable proposition) into a bone mill. The bones of the Maori dead in the caverns around about furnished ample 'raw material' for his enterprise. The tower of this unholy structure still stands, a silent testimony to its 'hardy pioneer's' energy". See "Human Bone Dust", *NZF,* August 1893: "England is said to be the greatest consumer of human bones for fertilizing purposes . . . Already she has turned up the battlefields of Leipsic, of Waterloo, and of the Crimea".

16. Interview, Alf Skelton, Auckland.

17. Held by OKM with inward correspondence and share register.

18. *Annual Report,* Dept. Ag., 1907, W. Jaques, p214.

19. Handwritten, Warren Butterworth.

(5) *THE COUNT*

1. W. B. Souter, Two Pioneer Families, typescript 1959, author's collection.

2. Interview (and silver tea service), granddaughter Barbara Souter, Auckland.

3. Archives Historique, Paris, quoted by Souter.

4. *The Albertlanders.* See also *Paparoa-Matakohe Centennial.*

5. Buller, *Forty Years in New Zealand.*

6. Souter history.

7. Three vols. photostat, John Linnell, Tamworth, NSW.

8. The present owners, Owen and Mary Stevens, have carefully preserved this room. The house was spared a move from the water because an early owner was county engineer R. J. Baff — a man well placed to have a long access road put in.

9. Interview Mollie Stevens, Ruakaka.

10. Letters held by John Linnell.

11. Death certificate. The Souter history, not always reliable, gives cause of death as pneumonia. According to a granddaughter he was an epileptic.

12. *King William's Tree,* County Down brochure reproduced by Souter.

13. "Cloon Eavin" in *Burke's Landed Gentry.*

14. W. Davenport Adams, *Dictionary of English Literature.*

15. Lineage from *Dictionary National Biography,* with thanks to John Stacpoole.

16. Interview Owen Stevens and others.

17. Cemetery records, Otamatea County Council.

18. A 1913 photograph, often reproduced but anonymous, of a mounted baton-carrying figure in oilskins has come to represent the archetype of rural punitive force. Snelling's daughter, Mrs. K. L. Forrest Brown, identifies the subject as her father.

19. Interview Kate Melville, Auckland, who has family tree.

(6) *NO PICNIC AT PURIRI POINT*
1. Interviews Tom, Tosti (Mrs. Tait) and Frank, Auckland; Bill, Te Kopuru; Bernice (Mrs. Goodwin), Dargaville; and Vance Pook, Pahi.
2. Still in Maori ownership. The inland Latimer block of 150 acres developed by Maori Affairs was recently sold to the adjoining Perkins Farm.
3. *Matarere* was lost by fire off Great Barrier, 1960. Her steam engine is displayed at Motat.
4. Held by Vance Pook.
5, 6. Interview Nell Beatson, Auckland, who says "Page Point" is properly spelt Paige, the original settler's name.
7. Interview, Mohi Manukau, Helensville.
8. Interview, Ian Hanna, Whakapirau.
9. It can. But it is also the name of that most graceful of Kaipara seabirds, the V-winged Caspian tern.

(7) *ALWAYS A PICNIC*
1. This anecdote, like the bulk of the chapter, is from family sources. Five relatives or close connections of Stevens were interviewed but in view of the painful circumstances direct attribution does not seem appropriate.
2. Massive limestone outcrops on the property were Maori burial places.
3. Still so well hidden it has escaped the Historic Places Trust listing that it merits.
4. The only original item in a house that is being sensitively preserved by the present owner, Ted Trembath. Previous owners sold the chandelier, later destroyed in a fire.
5. Interview, Vance Pook, a later *Nautilus* owner, given information by Lowe's son.
6. Information John Stacpoole, a Chadwick descendant.
7. Blackwell papers, Billie Guinness, Auckland.
8. Brian Muir, the applied arts curator's description.

(8) *THE BLACKWELLS*
1. Notes to family tree compiled by a grandson, Frank Blackwell, Wellington. Karepo was originally Maori reserve. See note 18, chapter 1.
2. Interview Les Wilson, Paparoa.
3. Diary held by Frank Blackwell.
4. Blackwell papers, Billie Guinness, Auckland.
5. Held by Barbara Skelton, Auckland.

6. Source untraced. Author invites enlightenment.
7, 9. Rev. T. F. Robertson, *NZH* supplement, 7-7-1906.
8. 26 May 1906.
10. Cheeseman letters, Auckland Museum Library.
11. Communication Dr. Robert Cooper. Information from G. V. Hudson, entomologist, who was present.
12. Volume 5, number 1, 1962.
13. Vera Moreland letter 5-12-1977 quoted Botany Division DSIR *Newsletter*, December 1985.
14. When Frank Blackwell Jr. died (at 38) Hall Skelton conducted the service. *Rationalist*, October 1941.
15. Papers, Frank Blackwell.
16. Papers, Billie Guinness.

(9) *A PARTY OF ONE*
1. A life appointment. In 1891 new members were given 7-year (renewable) tenure.
2. *PD*, 6-11-1903.
3. Cole-Catley, *Springboard for Women*, 1986.
4. Published Wellington, 1888. His earlier work, *The New Zealander on London Bridge or Moral Ruins of the Modern Babylon* by MLC, was published in London, 1878.
5, 6, 7. *PD*, 15-6-1906, 8-4-1897, 29-9-1899.
8. *Paparoa-Matakohe Centennial, 1862-1962*.
9. *PD*, 7-7-1910, 3-8-1910. Scotland thought working men should look after themselves and later supported protection only for women and children. And yet he opposed a wife assault bill as one-sided. What if a hardworking husband comes home to be beaten with a broomstick by a drunken wife? he asked. Perhaps he was prompted by his neighbours across the river: old Etonian remittance man, Sydney Cuthbert Rathbone, was regularly beaten by his wife Gretchen (Weber) on returning home — except that in this case it was the husband who was drunk. His family fortune came from the slave trade.

(10) *THE COATES FAMILY*
1. Sutch, *NZ's Heritage*, vol 6, part 79; Gardner, *An Encyclopedia of New Zealand*, vol 1. Dr. Sutch had almost completed a full-length biography of Coates when he died. His manuscript, filing cabinet of research material and masses of Coates family papers and photographs disappeared in odd circumstances. One

supposition is that after their unsuccessful prosecution of Sutch the SIS were anxious to deny him posthumous respectability — his approach to a conservative prime minister, tinged as it was with idolatry, would have seemed an unlikely one for a Russian agent. The suggestion may not seem so bizarre when it is remembered that the SIS attempted to interfere with the Sinclair biography of Walter Nash.

2. Watson, *Coates Centennial History 1866-1966.*

3, 5. Interview, Joy Aickin, Matakohe.

4. Interview, Alex P. Watson, Kaiwaka.

6. *AWN*, 29-1-1876. Memories of Anglican repression of non-conformists (the Coates were Anglicans) heightened feelings. An Albertlander descendant, Inez Hames, has written: "In Herefordshire, Lord Somers, disturbed that daughters only were born to him, was seriously advised that God might be punishing him for allowing Methodists to live on his estate. Consequently he ejected them all". *(Wesley Historical Society,* vol. 27 No. 5). In his 1922 recollections, Luther Hames tells of local feeling when the telegraph came through in 1879: "The Department laid out the line along the main road, Maungaturoto, Paparoa, Matakohe, whereat the group of gentry who used Pahi for a *centre,* brought influence to bear, and got the survey diverted to go through Pahi at the expense of a longer route and two cables. Paparoa democracy then rose in wrath at being unjustly cut out and held indignation meetings, etc. The upshot was a return to the original route, with a branch to Pahi. It troubled us not at all that Paparoa had only a telephone in a store, while Pahi got a specially built telegraph office and a salaried officer (who had very little to do)".

7. Copy, Shirley Tonkin, Matakohe.

8. Joy Aickin.

9. He gave Reischek "a really valuable present, the skin of the extinct dog *(Canus Maori)". (Yesterdays in Maoriland).* How packs of "dingoes" were hunted by Coates is described in *the Albertlanders.*

10. Joy Aickin.

11. Interview, Harry Liddle, Karekare.

12. *Auckland Star,* 23 November 1963.

13. Interview, Robert Sterling, Dargaville.

14. Interviews, Mohi Manukau, Helensville, Jim Gallie, Auckland.

15. Interview. Name withheld.

16, 17, 18. *PD* 26-10-1914, 21-8-1913, 18-5-1916.

19. Interview, Bob Efford, Ruakaka.

20. His economic views were demonstrated by crossing the chamber to congratulate Walter Nash on the first Labour budget. (Interview, J. P. Lewin, Wellington, who was present).

21. Farland, "The Political Career of J. G. Coates", MA thesis, 1965.

22. With many variants and passionate denials. A letter by Mrs. M. V. Sansom, *Auckland Star,* August 1974, details how Coates said this to her husband "over a glass of whiskey" in the Grand Hotel, Auckland. George Massey Sansom, a friend of Coates and foreman of a relief gang, had asked for a rise for his men. "It spoilt the friendship, on my husband's part at least".

23. Interview, Mollie Stevens, Ruakaka.

24. Interview, Dr. Kendrick Smithyman, Auckland.

25. Interview, John Barr, Auckland. From Ashwin tape.

26. Davis, *A Link With the Past.*

27, 30. Interviews, Clarice and Mavis Smith, Matakohe, Alex P. Watson, Kaiwaka, Joy Aickin and Shirley Tonkin, Matakohe.

31. John Stacpoole's sister was the nurse.

32. *North Auckland Times,* 3-3-1936, quoted by Farland.

33. Interview, Mohi Manukau.

34. King, *Te Puea.*

The Chadwick house, demolished 1958.

Illustration credits

Abbreviations: AIM — Auckland Institute and Museum Library. OKM — Otamatea Kauri and Pioneer Museum, Matakohe. *Note:* Glass negatives, Blackwell, deposited AIM, Gallie, deposited OKM.

Endpapers: Otamatea Regatta Club.
Frontispiece: Eugenie Withers, Auckland.

10 AIM, permission Otamatea Marae Committee, David Reynolds photo.
13, 19 AIM.
15, 17 *The Albertlanders.*
20 Rotorua Museum, on loan to AIM
21, 25, 28 OKM
23 Murray Gittos, Auckland
24 Jim Gallie, Auckland, George Gallie photo
26 David Simmons, Auckalnd
27 Detail from page 20
32 Alexander Turnbull Library
35 *The Albertlanders*
37 Author's collection
39 David Reynolds, Auckland
40 Alexander Turnbull Library
41 Author's collection
43, 44, 46, 47 Gwen Bryant, Dargaville
44, 45, 51 OKM
48, 53 Blackwell photos
49 Gwen Bryant; Trish and Ian Hanna, Whakapirau
50, 52 Mavis Bull, Auckland
53 John Linnell, Tamworth NSW; OKM

56 William Jackman, Auckland
59 Mavis Bull, Auckland
60 Fred Rathbone, Auckland
61, 71, 72, Blackwell photos
62 OKM
64 *Graphic,* AIM
66 OKM; Mavis Bull, Auckland
67 Warren Butterworth, Auckland
73 Author's collection
74 Alexander Turnbull Library
77, 82-84 Barbara Souter, Auckland
78 OKM
79 Onehunga Public Library
86, 90, 94 Tosti & Arthur Tait, Auckland
81, 91, 95 Tom Pook, Auckland
89 Norah Cox, Warkworth
96 Vance Pook, Pahi
97-102, 106 Eugenie Withers, Auckland
101 OKM (Percy Stevens)
102-105, 107 Ted Trembath, Paparoa
108, 117 Trish and Ian Hanna (Skelton Album)
110-122 Blackwell photos
123 Author's collection
124 Auckland Public Librery
126, 135 Alexander Turnbull Library
127 Author's collection
128, 129 Blackwell photos
130, 131 OKM
138, 152 Alexander Turnbull Library
139, 143, 146, 149, 153 OKM
141, 142, 143 Joy Aickin, Matakohe
145 Mary Hamblin, Marohemo
151 Jim Gallie, George Gallie photo

Index

Abrams, Constable Jonas, 69
Adams, Ernest, 62-3, 71
Aickin, Eleanor, 140, 142-3
Aickin, Dr. Thomas, 144
Albeitz, Wendolin and Ursalina, 62
Alderton, George, 30
Alexander, W. G. L., 70
Allan, Dr. H. H., 119
Ariell, W. W., 40
Ashwin, Sir Bernard, 150
Atkinson, Sam, 22

Bell, Dr. James, 16
Belshaw, Professor Horace, 150
Blackwell, Annie (Skelton), 113
Blackwell, Ellen, 109, 114-119
Blackwell, Frank, 109-123
Blackwell, Frank Jr. 116
Blackwell, John, 120
Blackwell, Nan (Annie), 113, 119
Blackwell, William, 109, 121
Blomfield, C. S., 70-72
Bragato, Romeo, 63, 65, 67, 69

Browne, Governor Gore, 11
Buller, Rev. James, 78

Campbell, Dr. R. M., 150
Casement, Sir Roger, 144
Casey, Captain J., 30
Castle, Amy, 119
Chadwick, John, 51, 77, 106
Chadwick, William, 38
Charters, Washington, 137, 141
Cheeseman, Thomas, 118
Clark, J. J., 40-1
Clayton, Susannah, 101
Clifton, Edmund, 71
Coates, Ada and Dolly, 141, 152
Coates, Edward, 50, 137-8, 140-2
Coates, Gordon, 55, 71, 92, 131, 137, 140, 144
Coates, Henry, 137, 142-3
Coates, Mrs. Marguerite, 148, 152
Coates, Rodney, 71, 142, 144, 150-1
Coates, Thomas, 50, 57, 68, 137-141, 151
Colbeck, Arthur, 61
Colbeck, Frank, 61, 131
Colbeck, William Henry, 20, 29-33, 57, 60, 78, 97
Colenso, William, 12
Cooksey, Samuel, 140
Cooper, Dr. Robert, 123
Creaghe, Robert, 68, 70
Cromwell, Oliver, 84
Cullen, Susanna, 16
Cuttle, Matilda, 113

Davis, Eliot, 151
Davis, Sir Ernest, 151, 153
Downes, Thomas, 42, 103
Dukes, Dr., 105

Eastman, Harry, 58
Edgar, Rev. Dr. Samuel, 53
Ewing (partnership), 31

Fairburn, A. R. D., 26
Fairburn, Edwin, 22
Fairburn, Frederick, 22-26
Fenwick, Stella, 121
Fletcher, Rev. Lionel, 112
Forrester, Arthur, 80

Gibson, Percy, 68, 71, 81-2
Gillies, Thomas Bannatyne, 25
Gittos, Esther, 22-26
Gittos, Kathleen and Sarah, 26
Gittos, Marianne, 11, 21
Gittos, William, 11-27, 50, 60, 62, 72
Grey, Sir George, 35-6

Gubb, Thomas, 24
Gulbransen, Mrs. Carl, 106
Guinness, Florence (Billie), 116, 122-3

Hadrill, Ebenezer, 51
Haines, George, 35, 78, 139
Hames, Luther, 39
Hargreaves, Joseph, 59, 62
Harihari, Janie, 92
Harris, Major Benjamin, 130
Hay, William Delisle, 57-8
Hayes, "Bully", 92
Herangi, Te Puea, 148, 153
Hika, Hongi, 12
Hill, Elizabeth, 80
Hill, Rev. John, 81
Hill, Robert, 77, 82
Hooker, Sir Joseph, 115-6
Hull, Francis, 80, 137-8

Isbister, John, 59

Jackman, Edith, 59, 69
Jackman, Eric, Ernest and George, 67
Jackman, Frank, 59, 72-3
Jackman, Guy, 67-8, 71, 73, 96
Jackman, Robert Ernest, 57-8
Jackman, W. Heathcote, 55, 57-73

Karaka, Arama, 15, 17, 20-1, 58, 61
King, Gilbert, 68-9
Kirk, Thomas, 115-6
Kitchener, Lord, 132

Labrosse, Ada Louisa de, 80
Labrosse, Augusta Caroline de, 80
Labrosse, Jane Isabella de, 75, 81
Labrosse, John Edgard de, 75, 84
Labrosse, Lionel de, 29, 75-85
Labrosse, Mary Augusta, de, 82, 84
Labrosse, Tyrell de, 84-5, 131-2
Labrosse, Violet Helen de, 84
Latimer, Sir Graham, 28
Laing, Robert, 109, 113, 116-9
Levet, Charles and William, 62
Liddle, Harry, 144
Linnell family, 47, 79, 84
Linton, John, 32

McConaughy, Isobel, 126
McConnell, Q. A., 70, 72
McLean, Donald, 13
McMurdo, H., 48, 65
Makoare, Mihaka, 139
Mander, Frank, 70
Mander, Jane, 8, 45, 101
Manukau, Kuki, 94

Manukau, Mohi, 91-2, 146, 152
Manukau Rewarewa, 13, 15
Manukau, Te Mate, 146
Martin, Nicholas, 55, 58, 82
Masefield, Joseph, 18, 32
Metcalfe, C. J., 57,77, 138
Metcalfe, W. H., 35
Monk, Richard, 61, 131
Mountaine, Dr. John, 50, 65
Mu, Pairama, 12, 68

Nathan, L. D., 38
New, George, 110
Ngapo, Annie, 146-7
Ngapo, Hohepa Hemi, 146
Ngata, Sir Apirana, 148
Nissen, Victor, 36-9

Oldham, Alfred, 38, 40

Paikea, Heta, 79
Paikea, (Te Hekeua), 13, 15, 17
Paikea, Pairama, 27
Paikea, Susie, 28
Pere, Wiremu, 133-4
Pharoah, Ada Grace, 100, 102-7
Pitney, B. L., 43
Pilgrim, Ada, 106
Pook, Bernice, 91
Pook, Edward, 87-96
Pook, Frank, 93, 95
Pook, John, 90, 92, 95
Pook, Kohinga, 87-96
Pook, Marina and Mary, 96
Pook, Thomas, 88, 90-93
Pook, Tosti, 88
Pook, Vance, 94

Quaife, Charles, 95

Ratana, Wiremu, 27, 92
Rathbone, Fritz, 148
Reischek, Andreas, 50
Riding, Rev. Abraham, 55
Rigg, John, 130
Robertson, Rev. T. F., 117-8
Rogan, John, 12
Rogan, Maraea, 146
Russell, Sir William, 85
Rye, Lewis, 57

Scotland, Henry, 10, 120, 125-135
Scotland, J. W. H. (Billie), 134-5

Seddon, Richard John, 128-130
Sellars, Captain Tommy, 55, 93
Shakespear, Percy, 82-93
Shakespear, John Talbot, 83
Sinclair, Keith, 19fn
Sinclair, Upton, 68
Skelton, Alfred Hall, 120
Skelton, Heber, 113
Skelton, Tom, 101
Smith, Brian, 51
Smith, Clive Kingsley, 121
Smith, S. Percy, 18
Smithyman, Kendrick, 150
Snelling, Douglas Cromwell, 84, 131
Stallworthy, John, 147
Sterling, Robert, 10, 134, 146
Stephenson, E. W., 103
Stevens, Alice, 100
Stevens, Elizabeth, 97, 100, 105-6
Stevens, Frank, 99, 107
Stevens, Gladys, 122-3
Stevens, Percy, 43, 100-1
Stevens, Sydney, 100
Stevens, Violet, 101
Stevens, W. H., 71, 97-107
Stevens, W. H. Jr. and Norman, 102, 104
Stoney, William, 55, 82
Sutch, Dr. W. B., 150
Symonds, W. J., 33, 61, 78

Te Whiti o Rongomai, 26
Thackeray, William Makepeace, 83
Tilby, Augustus (Bunnie), 89
Tipene, Wiremu, 12, 15
Toka, Henare, 27
Tonkin, Shirley, 150
Tuhaere, Paora, 18
Tyrell, Sophie, 76

Upton, William, 50, 112, 131

Waata, Piri, 18
Walsh, Austin, 34
Webb, Rev. A. W., 39
Webster, Geoffrey, 145
West family, 80
White, William, 12, 27
Whitmore, Sir George, 129
Wiapo, Andrew, 69
Wilford, Thomas, 148
Wright, James, 38-40